FAMILY RELIGION,

OR THE

DOMESTIC RELATIONS

AS

REGULATED BY CHRISTIAN PRINCIPLES.

BY THE

REV. B. M. SMITH,

PROFESSOR IN UNION THEOLOGICAL SEMINARY, VIRGINIA.

A PRIZE ESSAY.

PHILADELPHIA:
PRESBYTERIAN BOARD OF PUBLICATION,
No. 821 CHESTNUT STREET.

STEREOTYPED BY JESPER HARDING & SON, PHILADELPHIA.

ADVERTISEMENT.

A GENTLEMAN in the southern part of our country, in the earnest hope of more fully directing attention to the importance of the Family Constitution, proposed to give a prize of two hundred dollars for the most approved treatise on the obligations imposed by religion in the family, with particular reference to the present aspect of the subject.

The proposed prize essay was to be thrown open to competition, and the Presbyterian Board of Publication was selected, as the medium of communication, to publish the proposals, receive manuscripts, and determine the successful candidate.

Within the limited time, sixteen essays of various

grades of merit were received, and the following one was adjudged worthy of the prize. This essay exhibits a just appreciation of the great ethical duties involved in the discussion, and, as is believed, is written with more than ordinary vigour and freshness. It is submitted to the candid perusal of the reader with the hope that it may prove serviceable at a time when, through indifference or mistaken judgment, very erroneous views are entertained in regard to parental and filial duties. Were the relations which result from the family compact rightly comprehended and sacredly observed; the obligations resting on every family to reverence and worship God properly developed; and the practical methods of organizing households on a scriptural model forcibly illustrated, a new order of things might reasonably be anticipated. Reform in the family would soon diffuse itself throughout the whole constitution of society, a higher tone of morals would be inspired, and not only would the moral influence of the church be enlarged, but the stability and security of the state be perpetuated.

Whatever, therefore, may tend to arrest attention to this subject and enlighten the public judgment should be encouraged; and especially is it incumbent on the Christian community to promote the circulation of well digested views on the family constitution as lying at the basis of all that is excellent and praiseworthy in human society at large. These benefits, it is confidently hoped, will be promoted by the careful consideration of the ensuing treatise.

EDITOR OF THE BOARD.

TO THE

Memory

OF MY MOTHER;

THROUGH WHOSE PRAYERS, TEACHING,

AND EXAMPLE IN HER FAMILY,

BY THE GRACE OF GOD,

I WAS LED TO KNOW

THE TRUTH OF THE GOSPEL;

THIS VOLUME IS,

WITH TENDER RECOLLECTIONS,

AFFECTIONATELY INSCRIBED.

CONTENTS.

CHAPTER IV.

CHAPTER V.

CHAPTER VI.

INTRODUCTION.

THE Bible alone gives us an authentic account of the origin of our race, its earliest form of social organization, and the institution of the first means for its moral culture. "God created man in his own image; in the image of God created he him; male and female created he them." Gen. i. 27. "And the Lord caused a deep sleep to fall upon Adam, and he slept; and he took one of his ribs, and closed up the flesh instead thereof. And the rib which the Lord God had taken from man, made he a woman, and brought her unto the man. And Adam said, This is now bone of my bone, and flesh of my flesh: She shall be called woman, because she was taken out of man." Gen. ii. 21–23. "He which made them at the beginning made them male and female, and said, For this cause, shall a man leave father and mother, and shall cleave to his wife; and they twain shall be one flesh.

Wherefore they are no more twain but one flesh."—Matt. xix. 4–6.

Such was the foundation of the Family constitution. It was the first social organization, the germ and the pattern of all others. Adam and Eve constituted a family, and were thus constituted by God. As yet, there could be no civil government, no municipal laws, no magistrates and governors, and no provision for the exercise of any political power, for there were no subjects. Nor could there as yet exist an organized church, involving the idea of a ministry, the administration of sacraments, and the existence and operation of a government. Nor could there be any artificial educational institutions such as schools, academies, or other systems of instruction. Our first parents found within the limits of the family constitution, the essential means for securing to themselves and to their children, the benefits and advantages of government, school, and church.

Any other theory of the family constitution will prove to be a mere figment of infidel speculation. In the subsequent history of man, given in the Scriptures, we discover evident traces of just such a family constitution as has now been presented. With the increase of population other forms of social organization arose, but they preserved the characteristic features of this. The patriarchal system, which we find exemplified in the histories of Abraham, Isaac, and Jacob, is but an extension of the family. The "heads of the house of their fathers," (Josh. xxii. 14,) is an expression, which denotes the transition from an organization, of which the living family ancestor was the first in authority, to the more artificial arrangement, by which the government of a tribe or family connection was delegated to some other member. The frequent and familiar use of "house," for family, is another illustration of the position; and the municipal government, established by Moses, recognizes the principle of a family constitution, in the name and office of the "elders," whom he appointed rulers of the people.

So also an investigation of the most ancient and reliable uninspired histories of man, evinces the existence of the family constitution, as precedent to all other forms of social organization. It did not arise from any conventional compact. It was not the artificial arrangement of man, first living in herds, like the lower animals, and forming promiscuous and transient social relations, and thus gradually emerging into the order and permanent constitution of a well ordered household; but "from the beginning" the union of "one man and one woman," was established by God and ordained to be the foundation of an organization, which should be the unit and element and support of all others, for man's right government and culture. Indeed we may trace among the lower animals themselves, some evident indications of an arrangement somewhat similar. During the minority of their young, the parents instinctively unite in meeting the calls of that dependence which their offspring as instinctively feel towards them. A common speciality of nature, form, and habits pertains to the various classes of animals, and our use of the word *family* for designating such classes is a recognition of the facts, which illustrate our position. And not only so, but even in the vegetable world, there prevails a similar distinction designated by the same term. That such a mode of existence of the lower animals arises from the instincts of their nature, which prompts the dependent feeling of the offspring, and the protecting care of the parent, by no means sets aside our claims to the fact, as a teaching of analogy on our proposition; for these instincts are of God's ordering. What the Deist ascribes to the law of nature, we ascribe to the law of the God of nature; for there are no laws of nature, except those laws of God, by which he governs the natural world. What, therefore, we are taught in his word to believe to be the foundation of the family constitution, we might be led by the right exercise of reason, on the facts set before us, in the past and present state and order of nature, to conclude to be such.

When God had created man and established the family, "He blessed the seventh day and sanctified it." Gen. ii. 3. Moses perhaps alludes to this institution of the Sabbath in the use of the word "Remember," with which he introduces the fourth commandment. Ex. xx. 8–12. For, in the opinion of the best interpreters of Scripture, there are intimations to be found, in the patriarchal history, (cf. Gen. viii. 6–14; xxix. 27,) that the Sabbath was observed by the worshippers of God, and from Ex. xvi. 5, 22–29, it is very clear that its observance was required previous to the giving of the law at Sinai. We thus feel justified in understanding, by the terms used by Moses in the account of the institution of the Sabbath, that it was originally designed to subserve other purposes than that of a bodily rest. It was an institution for man's moral culture. Coeval with the family constitution, it was God's appointed means, by which the religious culture of the family should be promoted. It was a day selected and set apart from all others, as sacred to the worship of God, in which man, released from the laborious, though innocent employments of other days, might cultivate his spiritual nature and become perfect in holiness.

We do not know what would have been the methods of God's providence to the human race had Adam persevered in a state of innocence. It has been generally

2

supposed that, as just suggested, he would have become "perfect in holiness," and would have transmitted his holy nature to his posterity. Thus the multiplication of the race would have been that of holy beings. Inasmuch as Adam's son, born after the fall, was born in the image of his sinful father, (Gen. v. 3. Rom. v. 12–19,) such a supposition is not without reason. As Adam was created in the image of God, (Gen. i. 26,) an image consisting, doubtless, in "knowledge, righteousness, and holiness," (Eph. iv. 24. Col. iii. 10. L. Cat. Q. 17,) his descendants would all have thus reflected the holy image of the common Author of their being, at once illustrating his perfections and showing forth his glory. Thus by the combined agency of these two most ancient institutions, the family and the Sabbath, the world would have been peopled with a race of holy beings, who probably, by some suitable method, would have been transferred to some more permanent abode.

Whatever confidence may be reposed in these suggestions, which, however plausible, are neither articles of faith, nor essential to our spiritual edification, it must be conceded, that for the purposes of promoting man's continuance in primitive purity and happiness, the right observance of the Sabbath and the religious principles and practices of parents of families, fully imbued with the spirit of piety, would have proved very efficient. The use of means for sanctification would not be inconsistent with the Divine purpose towards man, any more than under the present dispensation. The peculiar means of grace connected with the gospel remedy, would not, of course, have been needed, and yet that "*holy* resting" of the Sabbath which is essential to an increase of holiness now, might have been equally demanded by the exigencies of sinless beings.

These are the only institutions of Eden, of which we have any account, which have survived the ruins of the fall. Though sadly impaired in all their elements of benefit to man, by that depravity of his nature, which often impedes the operation of God's most benevolent designs, and converts even blessings into curses, they still remain to us, in our fallen estate, at once the monuments of God's wise care for our welfare, and the valuable means for promoting our restoration to the purity and bliss of Eden. However much man has lost of the Divine image, in which he was created, these works of the Divine wisdom still remain "very good;" and even man's apostasy has not been permitted entirely to deprive him of their important aid to his moral improvement.

Of the aid which the family constitution is adapted to provide, it is our purpose to speak, in the following chapters. Following substantially the order of discussion prescribed by the benevolent gentleman who has called for this little work, we shall consider the nature, design, and importance of the family constitution; the duties and responsibilities belonging to it, as they pertain to the several members of a family, and are taught in the holy Scriptures; the best means to secure the ends, which appear, from a view of its nature, to have been designed by it; the relation which the family, according to its Scriptural constitution, bears to the church; the value, difficulties, and aids to family religion; and the pleas for neglect and delinquencies in family duties, offered by those who are indifferent or indisposed to their performance.

FAMILY RELIGION.

CHAPTER I.

THE NATURE, DESIGN, AND IMPORTANCE OF THE FAMILY CONSTITUTION.

SECT. I. *The nature of the family constitution.*

ACCORDING to the Scriptural account of the foundation of the family constitution, it consists, in its simplest form, in the marriage union of one man and one woman. Other members of the family are children, the fruits of such a union, and servants, transiently or permanently connected with this social organization. In a less accurate sense, other persons, temporarily inmates of the family residence, may also be included. An imperfect family organization is sometimes effected, when unmarried brothers or sisters, or both brothers and sisters are associated according to the principles, as to a common residence or common means of support, or both, which regulate the structure of ordinary families, so far as they are applicable to their peculiar condition. The death of either husband or wife does not necessarily destroy the organization of the household, though, of course, its efficiency is impaired, for the duties of both partners then devolve on the survivor; and as they are, in many respects, duties of very different nature, the whole cannot be as well performed by one as by both.

1. As the prime element of the family constitution is marriage, it is pertinent to our present purpose to offer a few suggestions touching the principles which should govern the formation of this relation.

(1.) Our Directory for Worship teaches, that "marriage is to be between one man and one woman only." Chap. xi. 3. Such was the law of its institution, "from the beginning," and such was, especially, reënacted by our Saviour. The union thus formed is obligatory till the death of one of the parties, unless there be a violation of the marriage vow by either, or that wilful and protracted desertion which implies the existence of such violation. Matt. xix. 4–9.

All theories and practices of men contrary to this fundamental law of marriage, whether by legalized polygamy, or concubinage, or by divorces for any other cause than that just stated, or some contingency manifestly implying its existence, or by any other avowed or unavowed evasions of the obligations of the married state, have arisen from the perverted judgments of men's minds or the depraved lusts of their hearts, and have resulted in evil, and "only evil and that continually," except when such results have been modified by the kind providence of God. Whatever views may be entertained of the violations of this law by the patriarchs and others to whose piety the Scriptures bear witness, it is a significant fact, that along with most of the prominent instances of such violation, of which a record has been given, there is also presented on account of some sad result, clearly traceable to such violation. The ill treatment of Hagar, the feuds and artifices of Jacob's family, the sufferings of Hannah, the domestic misfortunes of David, and the alienation of Solomon's heart from the service of God, seem to have been recorded as beacons. We need not discuss the various theories by which divines have undertaken to account for the facts to which we have alluded. God might, in the exercise of his sovereign authority, for wise reasons, suspend the law. Thus, in view of the disastrous wars which destroyed so many males, he may have been pleased thus to provide for a proper increase of population; or he may have permitted relations to remain undisturbed, though their formation was a sin, because greater evils might have resulted from their disruption. Or, what is more probable, in view of the record of evil results, such violations of the law were regarded by God as sinful, of which, however, his true servants may have been guilty, and for which they must have repented. That they might not have appeared to those perpetrating them so exceedingly sinful as they do to us, is easily explained by bearing in mind the state of morals among surrounding people, and the influence produced by the customs of others, on the sentiments of pious men. Our Saviour ascribes the toleration of divorce, as practised among the Jews, to the "hardness of their hearts." The record on which they based the custom of divorce, for trivial causes, was a permission not a command, Deut. xxiv. 1–4, and as the law required a formal separation, it was a testimony to the sanctity of the marriage relation.

But of the scripturalness of the law of marriage as we have given it, there can now be no doubt, on the minds of any, who receive God's word as the end of controversy.

(2.) As this important union is distinguished by such restrictions, and when formed, attended with momentous consequences to the parties, their friends, and especially the family to which it may give rise, it should be the result of a decided and mutual attachment of the persons, by whom it is formed. We do not mean to aver, that the want of such an attachment, at the time of marriage, so vitiates the relation, that the important and interesting results contemplated by it, are perpetually forfeited. For such attachment may afterwards arise; but should it never exist, or should one of the parties fail to entertain a true conjugal affection, there can be no such family constitution as the Scriptures propose. Such as arises from a union under these circumstances, is vitiated in a most essential element of success, in respect to the ends to be secured.

Without adopting the nauseating sentimentalism on this subject, which forms so much of the staple of tales and novels; we must on the other hand, express the conviction, that no persons can safely contract this union, unless affected by a decided and warm attachment for each other, based on a mutual respect and esteem, the results of a proper acquaintance, and the only satisfactory foundation of a true and lasting confidence. Such an affection by no means excludes that passion which draws the sexes together, but regulates its influence and subordinates its exercise to the higher motives, which should prevail in the selection of a husband or wife. Under its sole influence that personal attachment, which should be as perpetual as the marriage relation, and ever increasing, becomes a fitful caprice; violent it may be, but transient, and liable at any moment, to be superseded by the "expulsive power of a new affection" for some other object. Hence "love at first sight," and a precipitate marriage, often involve one or both of the parties in the miserable destiny of those who spend years of fruitless regrets, or by violations of the marriage vow, bring on themselves, their children, and their friends irreparable disgrace. Such marriages may, indeed, lead to favourable results, because the impressions of an hour may be confirmed by more intimate acquaintance; but, ordinarily, no rightly constituted family springs from such inconsiderate unions. Nor can such a family constitution as the Scriptures contemplate be expected to result from marriages of convenience or pecuniary interest, whether contracted by the parties themselves, or by others having a real or supposed right to control their choice. Whether increase of wealth, or enhancement of social position, or any similar reason induces the marriage, unless affection should afterwards intervene, most deplorable evils must result. The obliged party, whether male or female, will either become the abject vassal of the other, or mutual recriminations and perpetually growing estrangements will distinguish an intercourse, which should be that of affection and confidence, and infect in their sad consequences the entire family constitution, which may take its rise in the ill-fated union.

Among the causes of ill-assorted unions, the want of a

true Christian faith, on the part of either husband or wife, has been sometimes assigned, and the words of Paul, "Be ye not unequally yoked together with unbelievers," (2 Cor. vi. 14,) have been quoted to sustain this opinion. It is at least doubtful, whether the apostle had this relation especially in view. Supposing such to have been the fact, then it must be borne in mind, that the "*unbeliever*" among the Corinthians, was one who openly and profanely rejected Christ. By us, it is used in the wide sense, so as to denote any non-professor, and it may be questioned, whether the prohibition, admitting that it refers to marriage, would be correctly interpreted, so as to make the marriage with any other than a professing Christian, scripturally unlawful. Many such "*unbelievers*," though, alas! truly "out of Christ," are persons of good morals and pious education, and are respectful hearers of the word, who may be "won by the conversation," or pious conduct, of a Christian companion. Still great caution need be used in selecting a partner for life, from among those who are not the professed people of God: and certainly a selection of such as are notoriously profane, drunken, or debauched in any way by sinful lusts, must materially mar the family constitution, if not utterly destroy those agencies for good, with which it has been provided.

The space allotted to this discussion of the true doctrine of marriage, should not be regarded as disproportioned to the intrinsic importance of the subject. Indeed there are reasons for regretting that we cannot enter more fully on the discussion. For there are ominous indications that very loose views are increasingly prevalent in many parts of our country; and there is a strong tendency manifested, to set aside the ordinance of God for the commandments and traditions of men. The increased facility with which divorces may be obtained, on very trivial grounds; the frequent violations of the marriage vow in the influential stations of society; the notoriously glaring and publicly advocated violation of God's law, by a whole community, in one of our Territories; and the licentiousness, which, open or concealed, marks the character of many schemes of professed improvement; all together call on all who love the welfare of our country, to lift up a warning voice, and rally around this divinely inspired and fundamental law of the family constitution.

2. We have seen (p. 10) that the family, as originally constituted, offered to its members the advantages of a school, a government, and a church. Notwithstanding the sad change in man's relations to God, by his fall from an estate of holiness into that of sin and misery, a proper family constitution is still, essentially, an organization for government, and secular and religious instruction.

(1.) In the law prescribing the relation of Eve to Adam after the fall, she was placed under his authority. "He shall rule over thee." Gen. iii. 16. Such was evidently the normal relation of the wife in all those families, of which a history is given in the Old Testament, and such is the purport of apostolic teaching, when inculcating the duties of wives. Col. iii. 18. 1 Peter iii. 1. By the terms of the fourth and fifth commandments, children and servants are recognized as subject to the father and master, (L. Cat. Q. 124;) and in the fourth, even "the stranger," within the family precincts, is placed in a similiar subordination. These teachings of the Old Testament are also confirmed by those of the New. Here then is an organized government, the authority of which is vested in the husband, father, and master. The subjection of the wife is not, indeed, of the same sort as that of the children and servants. She is the partner of her husband as well as his subject, identified with him in a common interest and in their common relations to others. Thus our Saviour teaches; "they are no more twain but one flesh," Matt. xix. 5, and Paul says "men ought to love their wives as their own bodies: he that loveth his wife, loveth himself." Eph. v. 28. The children are required to obey their parents, (Eph. vi. 1,) the mother, as well as the father; and the obedience to masters required of servants (vi. 5.) implies the obligation to render it to mistresses. Still it is a significant fact that in the very connection in which Paul teaches the identification of husband and wife, he explicitly asserts that the "husband is the head of the wife," that wives "should be subject to their husbands in every thing." Eph. v. 23, 24.

The government of the family is then a monarchy. But though a monarchy, it is not necessarily a tyranny. For the law which prescribes the subjection, modifies it very materially, by two limiting enactments. Husbands are required to love and cherish their wives, deal tenderly with their children, (Eph. vi. 4,) and justly with their servants, (Col. iv. 1,) and the obedience exacted of the subjects of this government is to be rendered "in the Lord," *i. e.*, in a Christian manner or on Christian principles; and of course the family ruler must exact that obedience in the same manner.

Cases may occur, in which this supreme power necessarily devolves on the wife; as when the husband, by reason of bodily or mental infirmity, is manifestly incapable of its exercise; and, of course, when he may have been removed by death. There are also, in our sinful world, but too many instances of its abuse. The head of the family sometimes becomes its oppressor, so that wife, children, and servants are made the victims of ruthless acts of passion and caprice. In view of such cases, there are those who are disposed to ascribe the lamentable evils which are suffered to the institution itself. But it has been found impossible to construct a substitute. Even when human laws have undertaken to remedy some of the lesser evils flowing from badly governed households, they have, but too often, occasioned greater than they relieved. The evils of which we complain are due to sin, not to the institution itself. If to remove them, it be abolished, we shall find that we have also destroyed an agency for good. It is better to content ourselves with the structure which God has raised, even though its beauty be marred by sin, than by its destruction to bring on ourselves even greater calamities, to which our necessarily imperfect substitutes must be equally or more liable, and to which they will offer but little compensatory benefit.

It deserves our remark, however, that the family constitution is no less a government when that government is badly administered. Of the responsibility which that fact imposes on those who rule, and the results involved as to those who are ruled, we shall have occasion to speak elsewhere.

(2.) As an organization for instruction, both secular and religious, we find in the family constitution, teachers and pupils, subjects, opportunities, and methods of instruction. It is a school in the widest sense, and in this aspect of its nature alone, is suggestive of many interesting considerations. As in the government, so in the instruction of the family, the husband and father is the head. To him the wife (1 Cor. xiv. 35. 1 Tim. ii. 11, 12) must look for needed religious information, and to him specially, the Scriptures address admonitions to the duty of instructing as well as governing the children. Still the wife is his associate as well as pupil. Thus both parents are teachers, and whatever be their character and that of their instructions, must be efficient. On the minds and hearts of their pupils, for the most part their children, they may make the earliest and most durable impressions. Their teaching may not be of a very high intellectual character; and yet even in this respect, their moral qualifications, arising from the instincts of parental affection and their relation to the child, together with the opportunities they enjoy of giving early and repeated lessons, confer on them great advantages for a successful communication of knowledge, and a beneficial mental training, to the extent of their own abilities. And then by their example, daily admonitions, and advice, they are capable of exciting their children to greater activity and eagerness for mental improvement. There are many mental habits of great importance to the successful efforts of a student, in which parents, of even moderate intellectual attainment, are the most efficient trainers. As already intimated, we must also bear in mind, that the process of instruction begins at the earliest possible period. The mother's chamber is the best infant-school room. The parent has access to the mind and heart, before the faculties of the one have been injured by injudicious modes of culture, and the affections of the other have become set on that which is evil and alienated from that which is good. In early life, children are more susceptible of instruction in things than words. They are naturally inquisitive, credulous, and confiding. But they are volatile, and incapable of protracted mental effort of any kind, and especially, of processes of reasoning. Then is the period for imparting the knowledge of important facts, and for making impressions of useful truths; and for such a work, no one is so suitable as the parent, who can listen with unwearied patience to the prattling questioner, with a tender regard for the child's best interests will aim to fill the opening mind with unmixed truth, and, by a variety in the matter and modes of teaching, will adapt it even to the fickle temper of childhood. It is especially in regard to moral training that this fireside teaching evinces its superiority to any other. The daily and almost hourly opportunities of the parent for inculcating love of truth, the practice of self-denial, and the exercise of forbearance, gentleness, and kindred virtues, and of correcting tendencies to evil, checking the ebullitions of temper, and curbing propensities to the indulgence of malice, envy, and similar vices, afford an advantage for such culture, no where else to be found, even could as suitable teachers as parents be procured. And just those methods of teaching which the companionship of children and parents dictates, are just such as the peculiar circumstances of the former demand. Moral principles and habits must be inculcated by continued and frequently repeated efforts, by little and little, rather than by set forms of admonition and protracted lectures. To the former it is obvious, that the age and employments of children peculiarly fit them, while they render the latter as certainly unsuitable.

The remarks already made supersede the necessity of any special suggestions touching the suitableness of this school for instruction in the manners and minor morals of life. The same considerations which have been offered as to the more important departments of instruction, apply in respect of these. So also in whatever relates to the physical education, not only of those of very tender years, but also of those of riper age, the parents, as the natural guardians of their children, possess a peculiar suitableness for giving instruction and inculcating useful habits.

But parents are not the only teachers of this home-school. Children become teachers of children, and servants and dependents may be, in turn, teachers and taught. Parents themselves are in a school, where experience presides, to confirm the lessons which duty, instructed out of God's word, imparts; and whether for good or evil, there are ever going on, in ten thousand of families, processes of mental, moral, and physical training, which precede in time, and often in efficiency, those more artificial agencies, which are employed to mould the character and shape the destiny of man. Where the family constitution includes servants in the organization, we have a happy exemplification of its capabilities for that instruction, which is most essential to the welfare of all, and of which, by their circumstances in life, such persons stand most in need. We mean, of course, religious teaching. Like children, servants are under authority. To a certain extent, of which we may have more to say hereafter, their religious training is in the hands of the master. Their necessities, in this respect, are by no means represented by their desires. On the contrary, the less they have, the less they desire of religious influences. As belonging to the class of the ignorant and poor, they are dependent; and yet, left entirely to themselves, they would rarely seek knowledge. But as parts of the family, they are, especially while young, in a position eminently adapted to secure for them the advantages of moral training. Many of the privileges which children enjoy, in respect of daily intercourse with those who teach, the influence of example, the reiteration of practical lessons on virtue and vice, and the useful restraints to which they are subjected, are, to a great extent, those of servants; and it is doubtful whether any method could be devised, by which this class of persons, free or bond, would have extended to them better means for religious improvement, than those afforded by a well ordered family constitution.

While, in our remarks, we have had in view the nature of this constitution as established by God, we are not unmindful of the fact, already intimated, in speaking of it as a government, that by reason of man's depravity, it is not by any means necessarily a school of righteousness, of useful learning, nor even of proper physical training. Still, even if a school of opposite results, it is no less a school, and whether for good or evil, one of the most important agencies which God has employed for bringing blessings on man, or which man has perverted to bringing curses on himself.

SEC. II. *The design of the family constitution.*

A discussion of the designs of God in organizing the family constitution will serve to illustrate and confirm the views of its nature now presented, and will also bring to our notice, others which are necessarily involved in such a discussion.

(1.) A prominent part of this design was the multiplication of mankind. The injunction given to our first parents before the fall, (Gen. i. 27–8,) was repeated to Noah and his sons, after God had destroyed all the rest of the race for their wickedness. That the purpose of this injunction or (if any prefer the word) permission, was ordained to be effected by marriage, the fundamental element of the family constitution is clearly implied by the circumstances under which it was originally given, and the emphatic statement of Moses, that of all women, only the "*wives* of Noah and his sons," were saved in the ark. Physiologists, statists, and the soundest political economists and moral philosophers confirm this view, by a concurring testimony, that, other things being equal, marriage is the best means to effect the purpose of the divine injunction.

(2.) Intimately connected with this, another part of the divine design was to secure the preservation and bodily welfare of children. Let none suppose such a purpose beneath the attention of the all-wise Creator. Although man's immortal part far exceeds, in value, his mortal, yet while on earth the sound condition of the intellect and the affections is so intimately connected with that of the body, that the right development of the physical constitution is materially subservient to the cultivation of man's nobler faculties of soul. He, therefore, who does "all things well," and cares even for the sparrow, has provided for securing to the human race, as much bodily health and vigour, as is consistent with man's fallen estate.

The infant of the human species, it has been often observed, is the feeblest of all animals at its birth, the least provided with instinct and the least capable of preserving its own being. Hence it needs the tenderest attention, the most assiduous care, and the most untiring perseverance on the part of others, to develop its physical faculties to a mature exercise. And long after the young of other animals are able to provide for their own wants, must children still be objects of watchful care for their health, their food, clothing, and comfortable lodging. Now God has designed, by the perpetual and exclusive union of their parents, exactly the most appropriate means to secure the care and attention to children, of which they thus stand in need. By neither alone, could the duties required be adequately performed. Although, the mother, in common with some other animals, is provided in her own body, with the most suitable nourishment for the infant, and, in common with all, led by the instincts of nature to extend to her helpless offspring a tender and watchful care, in the performance of a thousand nameless, but essential acts of kindness, which no hireling could be induced, however capable, properly to discharge; still unaided, she must ordinarily fail to meet the full demands of her position. The long and feeble state of infancy is itself a severe exaction on her strength, her time, and her health. The care of other children and a provision for their many and increasing wants would devolve on her yet heavier responsibilities, and exact severer toils; and thus must she either put in jeopardy the health and lives of her offspring, or sinking under her burdens, leave them, perhaps to a harder fate, in the hands of others. On the other hand, although the father might be more capable of sustaining the burden, which the support of older children imposes, he is, by the nature of those duties, in the performance of which he finds his capability, all the less fitted for the care of infancy and feeble childhood. Thus the deficiencies of one parent are supplied by the other, and in their combined services we see the wise and benevolent design of God toward children beautifully exemplified.

Farther, let us briefly notice the influence on the physical condition of the race, resulting from a relaxation, neglect, or violation of the scriptural law of marriage. In heathen and other lands, wherein either or all of these evils exist, we find that a physical degeneracy or loss of population, or both, have followed. A regard for common welfare and the evidently destructive tendency of licentiousness have given rise to laws, or customs with the force of laws, among all such nations, the operation of which has served partially to prevent or remedy the sad consequences which must have otherwise ensued. Indeed we may find among some, that the "law written on the heart of man," has preserved a great measure of its authority. Still, where the light of the gospel has never shone, mankind only yield such obedience to the laws of conscience as suits their interests, and the cases of its palpable violation often become so numerous that a state of transgression is rather the rule, and that of obedience the exception. Polygamy, concubinage, easy divorce, and incest, with their consequences, infanticide, exposure and desertion of children, and neglect of their most necessary wants, clothe the domestic histories of such nations with some of the darkest features of man's degradation. And in nominally Christian nations, how often does the indulgence of vicious propensities impair or destroy parental instincts! Sin and shame soon efface the lines of duty to children, written on the heart, by the finger of God, so that the mother forgets her tender offspring, and the father denies and spurns from his sight his own blood.

These remarks suggest another testimony to the adaptation of the family constitution, for the continuance and preservation of our race. Many schemes of benevolence have been devised to provide for those children, who have been deserted by poor or vicious parents. In the largest and best arranged establishments of this kind, we have reason to believe the best medical skill and the best nursing available are employed, and yet the proportion of deaths is far heavier than among the infants which enjoy family care. Homage is rendered to the family institution also, in the fact, that while, on economical grounds, the youngest infants are cared for in common, at the earliest possible period after infancy, the children are placed in suitable families, to enjoy the peculiar physical as well as moral benefits which they offer. However much, then, we may admire that benevolence, which thus provides for those innocent sufferers by the sins or misfortunes of others, we are constrained to feel, that the teaching of the experiment sadly demonstrates man's incapacity to improve God's plans. Indeed it has appeared that the success of such institutions has tended to increase the crimes, the evils of which they were in part designed to prevent or alleviate. God has thus sanctioned the family constitution, by not allowing man's best intentioned and best devised schemes for ameliorating the evils which flow from despising it, to be unmixed blessings.

Whether then we consider the adaptation of this constitution to the preservation of a healthy race, or the failures in this respect which follow its neglect, we are equally confirmed in the position, that this is one of the important ends which God designed in its organization. To the same purport, did our limits permit, we might adduce a testimony from the long train of evils to man's physical condition, incurred by those, who perpetuate crimes against the marriage-law, evils which enfeeble the body and taint the blood, and are transmitted with vitiating power to posterity, involving also, in their train, the most deplorable influences on man's mental and moral condition.

(3.) Another design of the family constitution is the promotion of true piety. Its eminent adaptation to secure such an end, is a fair inference from the considerations of its nature already offered. The authority of the parent and the subjection of children and servants, the early, frequent, and long continued series of opportunities for giving and receiving instruction, the confidence of children in parents and the natural concern of parents for children, the oft recurring occasions for bringing the great truths of the gospel to bear on the affairs of practical life, are some of the prominent and more obvious considerations, which induce the inference, that an organization evincing such an adaptation for promoting religious knowledge and practice must have been thus designed by its Author.

Again, the truths of religion which men are most concerned to know and receive, are those which address the faith rather than the reason. All such truths must first be received on authority. They are revealed by God, and are therefore to be believed by us. But it is all important, that those whose faith in such truths is demanded, should have confidence in those who present them as divine revelations. Now children instinctively give credence to what their parents tell them. When we remember how slow a progress the gospel makes among adults, who have had no religious training, and how the cares of this life and the deceitfulness of riches choke the growth of good seed, we can but admire the wisdom of that plan, by which provision is made for securing to truth an effectual lodgment in the mind, before the corrupting and alienating influences of the world have attained full sway.

The duties of true piety are coincident with the duties

which parents ought to press on the minds of their children, in view of their temporal welfare. While acting fully up to those requisitions, which the nature of the family constitution as a school sets forth, the parent is also training his charge for God's service.

The privacy and quiet of the family, its seclusion from the noise and bustle of society, and its comparative exemption from the intrusion of occasions of temptation, together with the limited number of the pupils and their intimate relations and friendly intercourse, all mark the fireside as a most favourable spot for inculcating and receiving those truths, which make wise to salvation.

Finally, the teachings of the word of God are conclusive on this topic. We need not advocate, as has sometimes been done, the proposition, that the family constitution is, in any proper sense, a church. The idea is not countenanced by Scripture. Even were we to interpret the apostle's phrase, "the church that is in their house," Rom. xvi. 5, to denote a family organized into a church, it would not follow, that every Christian household is a church. Nor is there any reason to suppose that such a title was used as to the family of Aquila, except to designate a Christian assembly, accustomed to convene at his house. Although not such a religious institution as the church, the family is a religious institution, according to the Divine economy, which historically precedes the church and enters, as a unit, into its composition. Conf. of Faith, xxv. 2. Form of Gov. ii. 4.

For while there may not be found any passage, which states this proposition in express terms, we can clearly perceive that it is fully implied in many parts of both the historical and preceptive portions of Scripture. In the recorded recognition of Abraham's piety in his family, God intimates, that the fulfilment of the great promises made to him, and to mankind through him, was suspended on the religious character of his family;—"he will command his children and his household after him; and *they* shall do justice and judgment, *that* the Lord may bring upon Abraham that which he has spoken of him." Gen. xviii. 19. Indeed while the promise to Abraham and his seed had a far wider scope of fulfilment, than was presented in the temporal and spiritual blessings of his natural descendants, it includes them and, more immediately, his near progeny. By his piety, his faith, and obedience, God was pleased to communicate blessings to Isaac and Jacob, and Jacob's family. It is also instructive to notice, that it was through one selected family of Jacob's natural descendants, that God provided a ministry for his church; and though the special enactments, providing that the priests should be the lineal descendants of Levi, contain much that is typical, the arrangement is suggestive of the idea, that along with accuracy in genealogy, there was also required a careful preparation of the youth, in the home of their fathers, for the sacred service to which they were destined.

There are numerous promises of blessings, in which children are specially included with their parents. "The mercy of the Lord is from everlasting to everlasting upon them that fear him, and his righteousness unto children's children." Psa. ciii. 17. "The Lord shall increase you more and more, you and your children." Psa. cxv. 14. And so they are connected in threatenings.

God declares he will visit "the iniquities of the fathers upon the children." Ex. xx. 5. Accordingly, parents are addressed as the representatives of their children in religious matters. The destinies of the descendants of Noah's sons were indicated in the terms of blessing and malediction addressed to their ancestors. Gen. ix. 24—27. So also the predictions of Jacob, though addressed to his sons as they were gathered around him, Gen. xlix. 1—26, were descriptive of the future fortunes of their descendants.

Under both the Jewish and Christian dispensations, we find that one of the seals of the covenant of grace has a special reference to the religious relations of the children. The circumcision of Jewish children and the baptism of those of Christian households, each contains an implication, that the parents, who thus ask for their children a Divine recognition as children of the covenant, engage to bring them up as such. And as the Jews were directed most assiduously to teach their children the great facts of their history and doctrines of their faith, Deut. xi. 19. Psa. lxxviii. 3—7. Prov. iv. 1—13; xxii. 6; so under the Christian dispensation, the religious teaching of children is distinctly set forth as a parental duty. Eph. vi. 4. In both the Old and New Testaments, these precepts are sustained by examples of the conduct of pious men. Thus Joshua determined for himself and his "house," to serve the Lord. Josh. xxiv. 15. David, after his public duties had been ended, returned "to bless his household," 2 Sam. vi. 20, in imitation of the pious custom of his father, in whose house was a "yearly sacrifice for all the family." 1 Sam. xx.

6. To these may be added the example of one of more ancient date, the patriarch Job, who " sent and sanctified" his children, "and rose up early in the morning and offered burnt-offerings according to the number of them all; thus did Job continually," or "all the days." Job i. 5. The pious Jewish parents who brought their children to Christ, to put his hands on them and bless them, only carried out a proper view of the religious duties involved in the parental relation; and the record of the young Timothy, instructed by his mother Eunice and his grandmother Lois, presents, doubtless, only one of many such examples, which the history of that period might have afforded.

Comprehended in the design to convey religious blessings by the family constitution, it might also be shown, was that of thus securing the best temporal benefits. Godliness is profitable for this life. The good Christian will be the good citizen, and while God has appointed the family constitution an eminently appropriate and useful means of bringing many sons and daughters to heavenly glory, he has also ordained it as the wisest method of training citizens for the commonwealth. But as this design is comprehended in the other, we need offer no additional illustrations or confirmations of the position.

SEC. III. *The importance of the family constitution.*

Without claiming for the family constitution a precedence of the church, as a more efficient institution for promoting man's spiritual welfare; or precedence of the state, as a more efficient institution for securing to man all the temporal blessings of good government; the sketch now given of its nature and design must lead every reflecting mind to a high estimate of its importance in providing a most essential aid to both of these great agencies for man's civilization. It is to the proper observance of the law of marriage that we owe purity of blood, and that certainty of relationship, which, both as a sentiment and a fact, exerts such wide spread influence on man's happiness and the healthful structure, peace, and order of society. The great poet of England's Commonwealth, in lofty verse, worthy of the theme, thus presents the fundamental relations of this law to the family constitution and its blessings:

> "Hail wedded love, mysterious law, true source
> Of human offspring, sole propriety
> In paradise of all things common else!
> By thee adulterous lust was driven from men
> Among the bestial herds to range; by thee
> Founded in reason, loyal, just, and pure,
> Relations dear, and all the charities
> Of father, son, and brother first were known!"
>
> Paradise Lost, iv. 750–757.

Those kind and tender family affections which are associated with the words, husband, wife, father, mother, son, daughter, brother, and sister, are the rich fruits of this divinely ordained social organization. In barbarous lands they are hardly known. They constitute the true ties, which give to the word Home its power. They invest it with the charms, which, irrespective of all physical attractions, render it the object of early, constant love, and the source of our purest earthly joys. These "relations dear" bind together the elements of society. Families become knit to families. Associations of place and time,—memories of childhood and youth, with all the endearing attachments to old homesteads, which, with a sweet and holy power, bind men to the country of their birth, flow as refreshing streams from the family fountain. Hence, true patriotism, noble, inspiring sentiments, deeds of heroic courage, and power to suffer and to labour in a country's cause, which have been the themes of history and of song, have taken rise. In the family, woman has been elevated and throned. In no heathen nation has she ever been assigned her true place. In Rome only, of all ancient or modern nations, not Christian, was she raised to any thing approaching her high office. But in Rome, she was rather either the mistress or the slave of licentiousness, than the priestess of virtue. For the virtues of one Cornelia, Roman history narrates the vices of a hundred Messalinas. With few exceptions, " home was a word dissevered from those high and holy associations," with which, by the family constitution of the word of God, it has been connected. Hence the true place of woman did not exist, for home is the empire over which she reigns, with love as the sceptre of her power. Had the family constitution given the world no other sentiments, than those which are associated with the words wife, mother, daughter, and sister, it would deserve our high admiration, as a source of power over human hearts. Not only does the state derive from this divinely established institution, a healthy, vigorous population, the true capital of a nation, but by means of its bonds the rights of property are defined and secured, and its transmission regulated. Erase the family from the structure of society, and our laws of property would lose almost all their force as well as propriety. The estates of intestates would be the prey of rapacity, and the establishment of wills be next to an impracticability. Incestuous connections would engender a feeble race of men, who would expend their only strength in feuds and broils. Might would make right, or anarchy and violence sap the foundations and overthrow the structure of society.

The increase of national is the aggregate of the increase of individual wealth. But individual energy and enterprise find few such incentives as are supplied by a desire to enhance the prosperity and happiness of wife and children. While, on the one hand, the ties of affection and love of home tend to repress aimless roving, and exercise a conservative power in securing the stability of the state; on the other, the desire to build up the fortunes of a family opens up the forests of uncultivated lands, explores the distant hidden mines of wealth, causes the wilderness to blossom and bring forth fruit, builds marts of trade, and widens the boundaries of civilization. In a word, to this wise device of the all-wise God, we owe the continued existence, the increasing growth, the energy, and the enterprise of the race. Marred as it has been by sin, it is still an element of the purity and prosperity of the church, and of the progress and power of the state.

CHAPTER II.

THE RESPONSIBILITIES AND DUTIES BELONGING TO THE FAMILY CONSTITUTION.

SECT. 1. *The responsibilities and duties common to all the members of the family.*

THE nature and design of the family constitution necessarily impose great responsibilities on the members of the household. As God has founded the family, he has also instructed us in his word, how we must act in the several relations of husband, wife, parents, children, brothers, sisters, masters, and servants, so as to secure, for ourselves and others, the benefits of this important institution, and avoid converting any of the elements of its organization into the means of injuring our own welfare or that of society.

On the husband and wife, or parents, in whose union, the family constitution takes its rise, and especially on the husband or father, there rests the heaviest responsibility, for its character and influence. He stands in immediate relation to every other member of the family. All are subject to his authority and dependent on him, and, of course, will be materially influenced, in character and conduct, by his principles and course of life. But even the youngest or most ignorant accountable member of the family occupies a position, by which he may contribute to promote or hinder the full efficiency of an institution, whose power is to be found, rather in the harmonious coöperation of all its parts, than in the special excellence of any one of them.

Before discussing the relative duties of the members of the family, we may properly urge on the consideration of all, a few general remarks :

(1.) For the right appreciation of our responsibilities, in every relation of life, and a faithful discharge of the duties we owe to others, we need the renewing and sanctifying work of God's Spirit. A new heart and humble faith in Christ are essential to a sincere reverence for the authority of God's word, in which our duties are inculcated. In even the best Christians, the remains of indwelling sin occasion great imperfection. Much more then, may we expect those to come short, who rely only on the guidance of instinct, the inducements of interest, or the imperfect code of human morality. We admit, indeed, that under the genial, general influences of the gospel, there are men, who very commendably perform many duties, both of public and private life ; still it is only to those, who regard the teachings of God's law which prescribes man's duty to those "of his own house," authoritatively and perfectly, that we can confidently look for the full exemplification of that conduct which the constitution of the family demands.

(2.) The necessary intimacy of the family circle often occasions some clashing of personal interests or presumed happiness. As this intimacy is one of the chief charms of domestic life, it should not be sacrificed, to avoid these incidental evils. On the contrary, let these occasions for subordinating selfish views to the good of others, be made the means for exercising self-denial, forbearance, meekness, gentleness, generosity, and kindred virtues. Thus each member will be more strongly bound to the others, and all learn that the happiness of each is the happiness of all. Nearly related to this suggestion is another. In the family constitution we have an excellent exemplification of what, in political economy, is called a division of labour. No human wisdom could better arrange an institution in this respect. That this arrangement may be most productive of prosperity, and of peace and order, each one in the household should studiously avoid interfering with the province of employment allotted to the other. Otherwise there will be confusion, blunders, imperfections, and constant failures. The meddling of a husband in the affairs of domestic economy belonging to the wife, or the interference of the wife with the out-door labours of the husband, tends to derange the entire constitution of the family, to occasion contention, and hinder success in both departments.

(3.) Let those who are not pious avoid hindering the piety of others. The relation of every immortal being to God rises far superior to all earthly relations, and the rights of conscience are of the most sacred character. The husband, father, or master, who steps in between God and the wife, child, or servant, to prevent either from his worship and service, is guilty of a daring act of rebellion against God, as well as of a petty tyranny over one of his household. So if the wife, by any of the means of influence over the husband or other members of the family, which she can exert, designedly holds such one back from access to God, she is incurring the Divine displeasure as well as the risk of ruining a soul. No authority with which any member of the family is invested, nor any legitimate relation existing in it, justifies such interferences. And here it may be remarked, that in those frequently recurring cases in our country, when different church connections are preferred by the members of a family, the utmost liberty of action should be allowed. This is consistent, as well with a proper zeal for each one's own preference, as it is with a cordial affection to those who differ. All those moral means proper to be used to affect the views of others, as instruction, suitable persuasion and the like, are proper; but the use of authority on the part of those possessing it, or of angry recriminations or revilings or ridicule, on the part of others, disturbs the love and order which should reign supreme in the household. In all this, of course, we are not understood as teaching that children or servants, who of whatever age are yet in their minority by ignorance, are to be left uncontrolled, as to the kind of religious worship they ought to attend. Our remarks relate rather to those adult members of a family, who are presumed to be capable of making their own choice as to religious matters. Meanwhile it is our conviction, that, ordinarily, in rightly trained families there will arise but slight practical difficulty in this whole matter.

SEC. II. *Responsibilities and duties of husbands and wives.*

1. In the family constitution, as already shown, the husband is "the head of the wife," Eph. v. 23, as

well as of the family; but not thereby necessarily a tyrant. For the authority with which he is invested, is to be exercised in love. "Husbands, love your wives, even as Christ loved the church and gave himself for it." Eph. v. 25–27. As Christ employs his authority over the church for cleansing and sanctifying it, so must the husband use his over his wife for her benefit, and that of their common family. This scriptural view of the sense in which he is the head, while recognizing him as ordinarily superior in capacity, for directing in the affairs of business, and especially in whatever pertains to the out-door life, forbids him to use his power, merely to promote his personal ease or minister to his caprices, at the expense of his wife's comfort. This general statement of the scriptural law is the basis of several specific suggestions.

(1.) The husband should be considerate of his wife's health and bodily comfort. He should aim to lighten her domestic burdens. He has command of the common resources, and should not grudge expense of time or money, to afford her recreation and all needed help. Let him remember, that, though home is her sphere and her empire, it is not her prison, though she "worketh willingly with her hands," and "eateth not the bread of idleness," Prov. xxxi. 13, 27, yet she needs rest. Let him give her his company, aid in her mental improvement, and endeavour, by his pleasant and cheerful conversation, to make amends to her for the long hours of her loneliness, when he is absent on his business, or the yet more tedious hours of occupation, amid the torturing and perplexing annoyances of little domestic duties and cares. Let him share with her that night watching over sick children, which opens so many early graves for mothers. Above all, let him be careful to use his authority fully to sustain hers, over children and servants. Though his inferior she is their superior.

(2.) The apostle, to the injunction, "Love your wives," adds in another place, "and be not bitter against them." Col. iii. 19. In this there is displayed a consummate knowledge of human nature. Men who are wearied and perplexed with business, disappointed by the unfaithfulness of agents, distressed by the treachery of supposed friends, or injured by the arts of enemies, often bring darkened brows and anxious hearts to their homes. In no humour to bear patiently any petty annoyance there, they too often yield to the temptation to vent the spleen of their sensitive spirits, in fretting and "bitter" words. We admit all which can be said in palliation of such conduct. But the wife is the last person to whom such words should be addressed. In her kind sympathies and soothing attentions, the irritated husband ought to find means of comfort. Let him not destroy this resource. Rather let him curb his spirit, and seek, by confiding to her his sorrows, to open the fountains of her tenderness. He will not seek, in vain, from a true woman. Or, it may be, that though all has gone well from home, there await his return some of those petty vexations, such as late meals, badly prepared food, cold rooms, or noisy children, for which his wife may be responsible to some extent. Still, let him consider how many palliations of all this may exist, and avoid the "bitter" word. And even should she so forget her place and interest as to open the bitter fountains of ill-nature,—let him, with manly magnanimity, forbear to aid in the unamiable employment.

2. On the other hand, the scriptural injunction, "Wives, submit yourselves unto your own husbands, as unto the Lord," Eph. v. 22; or, as it is elsewhere expressed, "as it is fit in the Lord," (Col. iii. 18,) presents the fundamental principle of the duty of wives. One passage interprets the other. Paul does not mean, in the first, that the obedience to the husband is to "be as devout and unconditional as that which she is bound to render to the Lord, but it is to be regarded as part of her obedience to the Lord."* In other words, it is the obedience of a Christian, "determined by religious motives." And as the husband's authority is to be exercised in love, so the wife's obedience is to be limited by Christian principle. Hence,

(1.) Although in the context (Eph. v. 24) this subjection is required in "every thing," it is implied, that nothing is required contrary to the Divine command. Neither as to those acts of personal conduct, nor as to the exercise of her subordinate authority in the family, may she obey any such requisition. And yet even in this refusal, there should be the manifestation of a Christian temper, or what might be termed a Christian disobedience. Every effort should be used to avoid a direct conflict, a positive, decided breach. Gentle and kind remonstrance, studious efforts to please in all else, a mild and courteous refusal, should characterize the wife's demeanour. If her husband be a Christian, misled and self-deceived for a time, he will thus perhaps be led back to duty; if not, he may thus be "won by the conversation of the wife. (1 Pet. iii. 1.)

* Dr. Hodge on Ephesians, v. 22.

Let her, by all means, temper her conduct with Christian grace, and avoid whatever is exasperating and insulting.

(2.) This obedience, in other matters, should be implicit, prompt, and cheerful. There may be occasions when it is required in things indifferent, as it respects Christian duty, and yet perhaps very trying to the temper of the wife. Thus, the husband may interfere in her appropriate sphere, in the household economy, or in her modes of dress, or some other similar matter. Let her by a kind, gentle manner endeavour to dissuade him from his position or modify his views, but, if unsuccessful, she had better submit. If evil ensues, the discovery that he is alone to be blamed, will do more to convince him of the error of such a course another time, than her persistent and obstinate resistance. This might, by arousing his pride, induce him to persevere in his wrong doing, at the cost of valuable interests to both.

(3.) We have said this obedience should be "prompt, implicit, and cheerful." This is the spirit of the injunction, "Let the wife see that she reverence her husband." Eph. v. 33. The feeling of reverence is composed of fear and love, recognizes the superiority of its object, and unites trust with obedience. The wife who reveres her husband, desires to please, by the performance of all duties, whether prescribed or not. Hers is not a mere submission which may be petulant, sullen, and even insulting, as that of a refractory slave; but a submission in disposition as well as conduct, to the spirit as well as the letter of command. She will endeavour to anticipate her husband's wishes, and not by mere personal caresses, or a lavish care for his dress or the gratification of his appetite, but by endeavours to promote his domestic peace and comfort, and relieve him of perplexing and annoying cares, subordinating her wishes and plans to his, will seek to make his home the centre of his affections and the life-spring of his happiness.

(4.) Contrary to these scriptural views of the duty of a wife, is that theory of an equality of the wife with the husband in every branch of domestic authority, for which so many "strong-minded" women and weak-minded men, in our day, contend. Did the theory lead to nothing more than its terms propose, a most deplorable amount of family feud and dissension must inevitably result. But as there cannot be a "united head," in any government, consistent with good order and peace, the practical result of this perversion of the Bible doctrine, must be the utter subversion of the husband's authority. There may often be found women of a pert, conceited temper, who fancy that they know best what is for their husband's interest in his business, and understand better than he the whole routine of domestic management. They accordingly "usurp authority over the man," (1 Tim. ii. 12,) and essay to direct his servants, thwart his schemes, and order him as if only a steward, in the purchase and sale of property, the cultivation of his grounds, the education of children, and the expenditure of money. There are occasional instances, in which the wife is really more sensible and capable than her husband; but one who is really such, will show her good sense and ability, by quietly leading her husband to her wishes, seeming to serve while she rules, and sustaining his authority though really directing its exercise. She will look well to the ways of her household, and manage its affairs in the manner which he should have adopted, had his abilities made him adequate to his duties. There is much jocular and loose talking, in all communities, as to the subordination of one or the other partner in the family, which had as well be let alone as "not convenient." But many serious and biting truths are spoken in jest, and we fear that the advocacy of this subversion of scripture order, is often an illustration. As such a subversion has its origin in the depraved and diabolical principles of pride, vanity, and self-conceit, so it will, sooner or later, produce the appropriate fruits of disorder, misrule, and insubordination. For even when it is best that the wife should lead, if her conduct is not that discreet course described above, it will have the effect of mistraining her daughters to attempt following her example, in cases neither calling for such action nor permitting the attempt, except at the risk of a disruption of all family peace and order.

In this connection, we feel bound to protest against all those specious proposals for reforming the marriage constitution, by giving to the wife the same rights of property and civil position which now pertain only to man. There may be evils incidental to the present arrangement, by reason of man's sin; but the proposed remedy for these evils would only entail greater. It is but a step towards divorce, or other, and even more pernicious, infringements of the provisions of the marriage law. We feel confident of its ultimate failure. But that failure may be produced, only after, and by means of the disastrous consequences it must produce on society wherever its insidious poison takes effect. Let our people, fore-warned, be fore-armed, against all who undertake to be wiser than God, and boldly attack the works of his hands.

3. While we thus see that marriage does not destroy the personal identity of the parties, and by imposing on each special responsibilities, requires duties peculiar to each, at the same time, the intimacy of the relation gives rise to a class of mutual duties.

(1.) We know a clergyman who has been accustomed to substitute in the usual exhortation, closing a marriage ceremony, a short sentence, of this purport, "Be ever to each other what you now are, respectful, affectionate, kind, forbearing, faithful, tender, and true." In this excellent summary, we have but another form of the wise admonition, that a married pair should continue to evince to each other the qualities, and pursue the conduct, by which the admiration of one and the favour of the other were secured before marriage. Let there be mutual respect for the person, opinions, tastes, judgment, and right habits of each. They bear the same name, have the same social position, are one in the eye of the law, and, ordinarily, enjoy a community of goods. The character and reputation of each is that of the other. The husband must see in his wife, "his own body," (Eph. v. 28,) and the wife, in the husband, "the head" to which she belongs as a body, as the church does to Christ. Let each then exercise to the other the sentiments with which *self* should be regarded.

(2.) In accordance with these general aspects of mutual duty, each should repose in the other entire confidence.

The wife should have no secrets unshared with the husband. Let her avoid forming intimate friendships unknown to him. Let no foolish woman, married or single, or as foolish, and often more wicked, man, estrange her from him even in thought. He is her nearest friend. Even should he prove unworthy of her confidence, she had better weep over sorrow in secret and seek no earthly counsellor, than incur the risk of raising a barrier between herself and her husband, and pave the way for fatally impairing family unity and peace.

It is said of the good wife in Solomon's inimitable picture, "The heart of her husband doth safely trust in her," (Prov. xxxi. 11,) and even should a wife not present a full example of her there described, yet let not her husband withdraw his confidence. United with the imperfections which pertain to our common nature, there will generally be found in women, properly educated and honourably trusted by their husbands, a fair average of discretion, industry, prudence, enterprise, and energy. Women may be inferior to men in the reasoning faculty, and deficient in knowledge of those business relations, which properly pertain to the province of men, in the arrangements of domestic economy; but they are endued with remarkable powers of intuition: and with faculties for discerning what is right or wrong, proper or improper, sharpened by a sincere regard for the welfare of her family, a wife of an ordinary sound mind is her husband's best counsellor. On matters of business, out of her sphere, she may, from ignorance, be incompetent to give advice on the ways and means best suited to secure success; but even in such cases her judgment on plans, the operation of which may be explained to her, will be worthy of consideration. On all those questions, however, which present alternatives of good or evil results, let the husband consult his wife, and this the more particularly, when the interests of her children are involved. Could some law be devised, by which no man's signature as security could be valid, without his wife's assent, we should hear less frequently of families reduced to poverty, to pay the debts of some reckless or fraudulent speculator, or the property of the honest and industrious but unwary citizen sacrificed, to meet the liabilities of some wily, artful intriguer who manages to evade the claims of justice and revel in luxury, while his victim is left to struggle through life harassed by debt and pinched by want.

(3.) Let each carefully avoid addressing the other in the terms of severe rebuke or reproach. By reason of many imperfections and infirmities, "it is impossible, but that offences will come." Luke xvii. 1. The spirit of the Lord's precept as to the treatment of an offending brother, is eminently applicable in the similar intercourse of husband and wife. "If thy brother trespass against thee, go and tell him his fault between thee and him alone." Matt. xviii. 15. Let this be done in meekness and tenderness, with long suffering and patience, and in the exercise of a forgiving spirit. Gal. vi. 1; Lev. xvii. 3. On the other hand, let each be ready to confess a fault when it shall have been brought to mind. "Confess your faults one to another," and, it is well added, as intimating the duty of the offended party, "pray one for another." James v. 16.

Most studiously should each avoid indulging a fault-finding spirit, in the presence of others, especially of children and servants. That man would be thought truly unwise, who would weaken the influence and authority of a steward, on whose discreet management of his estate, his prosperity depended. The wife is the steward of the husband. Let her not be lowered in the eyes of those, over whom her authority must be sustained for the common benefit. On the other hand, let the wife avoid the indulgence of petulance towards her husband. It is contrary to the injunction "to reverence" him, and if borne quietly, will degrade him in her eyes,—or if resented, will open wider breaches in confidence and affection. In both cases, the results of this evil are of the most deplorable character. The offenders themselves may, for a time, feel a questionable satisfaction in the sense of a kind of superiority; but the husband has acted cowardly in dishonouring the "weaker vessel," and the wife rebelliously, in insulting her "lord," (1 Pet. iii. 6,) and both have injured themselves. Eph. v. 23–27. Thus too they build up a household of ill-natured and misgoverned children and servants, whose indolence and idleness, unrestrained tempers and disorderly conduct, will destroy the peace, and waste the property of the family.

(4.) Let the husband and wife strive to lay the foundations of a "happy home" for children, by making home happy to each other. Home is the wife's empire. It is a dominion in which the gentlest, sweetest affections bear rule. Let her be a "keeper at home," as well as discreet and chaste (Tit. ii. 5) in her home. Thus as a "strong man armed," she will "keep her house," and the precious goods deposited in it will be safe. So let the husband by his presence, whenever possible, evince his appreciation of her society, and thus cheer her heart, and sustain and encourage her in her efforts to minister to his comfort. The husband who finds his chief happiness in the society of the street, the bar-room, or the club,—and the wife, who is a tattler and busy-body, "idle and wandering about from house to house," (1 Tim. v. 13,) will soon have no home worthy of the name or suggestive of the sweet associations connected with the term.

(5.) Above all, and as supplying a foundation for the richest enjoyment of this union, so rich in blessings, let the husband and wife strive to promote each other's spiritual welfare. If neither is pious, let them as "one flesh," with a common earnestness, zeal, and prayer, seek a knowledge of the truth, renewed natures, the forgiveness of sins, engrafting into Christ, the application of his righteousness, and the hope of everlasting life. If one be pious and the other not, with what earnestness and untiring effort should the "believing" partner seek the true sanctification of the unbelieving! Let such then watch every word and action, by which an influence on the spiritual welfare of the other, whether for good or evil, may be exerted. The interests of children, servants, neighbours, and posterity may be affected. If the house remain divided, its religious power may fall. Especially should the believing husband strive for the salvation of the unbelieving wife. Women have generally manifested stronger Christian tendencies and susceptibilities than men. The graces of Christian character grow up more readily in a nature, which, though equally depraved, is not so prolific of hardening sins as that of man. The woman, too, is more secluded from temptation, and enjoys better opportunities for cultivating religious tempers. But, perhaps, for these very reasons, it has been observed, that the woman, who utterly refuses all religious influences, and yields herself to the unrestrained indulgence of vicious principles or corrupt habits, becomes, not only more incorrigible, but more mischievous than man. Woman presides over all those little streams of influence which affect the manners and minor morals of society. A look, a gesture, a smile, or a sneer from her, may often effect more evil than man's best efforts can easily undo. Thus the husband, whose children are the daily associates of a mother, unaffected by the obligations of Christian truth, has an incentive to the most diligent endeavours for her conversion, over and above the affection with which she is regarded.

With some modifications as to the motives, the believing wife should, with equal zeal, strive for her husband's salvation. She may do more for the spiritual welfare of her children and younger servants, unaided by him, than he can, unaided by her; yet, his aid is all important to the full influence of religion in the family. It should be her constant effort, by a consistent christian example, to win her husband to Christ. She need not "usurp authority" over him, as his teacher, or affect a superiority even in the moral relations of the family; but let her rather, by the society into which she leads him, the careful and prompt performance of her duties, and, especially, a studious regard for his comfort and happiness in his home, show him that her religion is worthy of imitation. On the other hand, let the unbelieving partner not only avoid all opposition to the other, in respect of religious privileges, on the grounds already adduced, but even on those of self-interest. The cost of the religious privileges of a wife is more than repaid in the temporal benefit which they fit her to confer. Those husbands, who interpose obstacles to the gratification of a wife's reasonable wishes, in such matters, are injuring their own best interests; and wives, who endeavour to dissuade husbands from a proper attendance on religious duties, abstain from aiding them in sustaining family worship, or attending to the religious welfare of children and servants, should remember how much more costly are the pleasures of gaiety and dissipation than those of religion, and how soon the temporal welfare of the household will be destroyed, if the salutary restraints and incentives of religious principle and motive be withdrawn. Indeed, the wife, especially, should bear in mind, that she owes her position of influence, even to oppose religion, to the benign power of the gospel. Only where its light and saving truths are known, has woman been raised to the dignity in which God created her; and only by the prevalence of true piety among men, can she sustain any higher relation in the family, than that of a favourite servant, and a ministress to the pleasures of a capricious and licentious tyrant.

Lastly, should both be pious, then, indeed, are the duties of promoting each other's spiritual improvement converted into delightful privileges. They are "helpers of each other's joy." There then arises an advantage such as that of having within us two souls. If one be in darkness and doubt, the other may come to aid, with the sweet promises of the gospel. If one be disposed to wander, the other can come, to call back the wanderer. If one fall, the other is at hand to raise up and restore. If one need light in ignorance, the other can come with the blessed truths of Scripture. In short, it might almost be allowed us to regard marriage, as one of the means of grace, when the union is that of a son and daughter of the Lord Almighty. Though constitutionally the husband is the head of the wife, yet before God, they are equal. He ought to be able to teach her, to be her guide and comforter. Yet if the order in this matter be reversed, no evil consequences need be apprehended. Let then the husband and wife joyfully, hopefully, and constantly strive together for the "grace of life," that thus they may be fitted for their duties as parents, improve to the highest degree the advantages provided in the family constitution, and be fully meet for a higher, holier and eternal union among the ransomed of heaven.

When persons who have sustained the marriage relation, and been widowed, enter into that relation again, besides the duties which have already been suggested, others of a peculiar character arise. Without entering very fully into the subject, it may be enough to offer a few general remarks :

1. It is no infringement of the rights of a living husband or wife, to cherish a tender regard for the memory of the dead. Sometimes there arises a petty jealousy of the contents of the grave. The portraits of the once loved

dead are removed, and every allusion to them regarded as indelicate. This should not be. On the other hand, all invidious comparisons of the dead and living, should be avoided. Let the new marriage relation be formed with proper motives, and while retaining an affectionate recollection of the dead, husbands and wives may cultivate the tenderest regard for the living.

2. When mixed families of children are thus constituted, there will be a demand for the more diligent exercise of those graces of forbearance, forgiveness, and long suffering to which we have alluded. No principle can be stated, which will, perhaps, better meet all the requisitions of duty which may arise than this: that husbands and wives should endeavour to treat step-children as their own, neither on the one hand utterly neglecting them, through fear of producing conjugal alienation, nor on the other, lavishing on them the love due to their own neglected offspring. The position of a step-father or mother is one which demands great circumspection and prudence, but at the same time, one, which, rightly filled, may be made a source of invaluable blessing to all concerned.

SEC. III. *Responsibilities and duties of parents.*

1. To parents, next in importance to the formation of the marriage relation, is the birth of a child. Thus is presented a common object for their care, love, and sympathy. Few parents, even of the reckless and dissipated among men, or the gay and frivolous among women, fail to be favourably affected by such an event. To the little feeble, wailing babe, "from travail unto travail born," has often been assigned, in the providence of

God, an influence for the benefit of parents, which the admonitions and entreaties of friends, and the most obvious considerations of self interest, had failed to secure. From the birth day of the first born, many a husband has become a soberer and a wiser man, and many a wife a more prudent and discreet woman.

To all reflecting parents, this event presents many new and interesting topics for serious consideration. Their position in life becomes invested with a new dignity. They are no longer to live unto themselves. The instincts of parental affection call for assiduous care and attention, in providing for the physical welfare of the helpless object of their common love. Its unfolding intelligence suggests to them, that it possesses a spiritual nature, on whose proper development its success and happiness in life will depend. They will also be reminded, that the future history of their child, as read in that of other human beings, will be entwined in the destiny of others. It is ordained to influence as well as be influenced by them. On the family of which it has become a member, on kindred, friends, and society at large, and, perhaps, from some position of eminence in the state or the church, even on the nation and the human race, their child may be appointed to exercise a moral power for good or evil, which may be felt in widening circles of benefit or injury through time, and even extend into eternity. Paul and Judas, Calvin and Charles V., Luther and Henry VIII., Knox and Queen Mary, Washington and Napoleon, were once just such "infants of days."

Above all, are parents called to consider, that they

have introduced into being an IMMORTAL SOUL. Their child has begun an existence which will never end. The earth is to be burned up, the heavens to pass away, the elements to melt; "the sun shall be darkened, the moon shall not give her light, and the stars of heaven shall fall;" but this feeble little body contains a soul, which shall still live and will ever live growing in intelligence, purity, and holiness, or sinking in pollution and misery, amidst the darkness of eternal despair!

In connection with these and other such considerations, parents are admonished, that to them, by the ordinance of God, in the constitution of the family, has been assigned a most important part of the work, by which this intelligent and immortal creature is to be trained; and that with their faithful or unfaithful execution of this solemn trust, will, in a most important degree, be connected the happiness or misery of their child, and the good or evil, of which its existence in the world may be the cause.

The heavy responsibility which thus devolves on parents, and which few properly realize, is enhanced by some further considerations.

(1.) Whatever be the nature and extent of those duties to children, to which the parental relation gives rise, parents are, ordinarily, least qualified for performing them, at that period of the family history, when this fitness is most needed. The training and character of the first born child will materially affect those of the other children. The novelty of the pleasure which a lively, healthy infant brings to a house, as it begins to develop its physical and mental faculties, often proves a serious hindrance to a right appreciation of the duties which its presence demands, and the blinded love for their tender offspring, which all parents feel, may more easily mislead those sustaining the relation, for the first time, to form inadequate or erroneous views of those duties.

(2.) Such is the nature of the family constitution, that parents cannot properly delegate to others the responsibilities which their relation incurs. Whatever aid, in the performance of their duties, they may be able to secure, they remain solely responsible; and it is by no means a matter of small moment, in rightly apprehending their position, that they may greatly increase the difficulties of properly performing their duties, by the very aids which they select.

(3.) To parents belongs the office of making the first and hence, ordinarily, the most durable, and, often, the most important impressions on the child's character. The work of teachers begins later. Often, when the most skilful and successful, they fail to eradicate the plants of evil growth which have been fostered by imprudent, or permitted to grow by negligent parents.

(4.) The labour to be performed by parents is not that of a few days or months, but of years. The result is not to be accomplished by one special vigorous effort; but it is the consequence of many little acts. It is not by a few violent, though well directed, blows of the mallet which blocks off heavy fragments of the rude marble, that the sculptor succeeds in his art, nor by a few broad strokes of the brush, that the painter spreads on the canvass, the conceptions of his genius; but it is by the countless delicate touches of the chisel or the pencil-brush, no one, perhaps, producing any perceptible effect, yet each important, as an element for securing the designed result, that the one succeeds in presenting us the accurate, almost speaking model of the human figure, and the other transfers to the once naked cloth, the forms of animate and inanimate nature. So the parent, not by a few special acts or influences, but by the almost unconscious exercise of moral power, in word and gesture, in frown and smile, in tones and manner, as with daily touches of the moral chisel and brush, illustrating the "mighty power of littles," shapes the living soul for a place among the monuments of an ever glorious temple, or the scathed and blackened ruins of a lost world.

Nor must we forget, that this work is to be performed, amidst all the perplexities and trials of daily life, the interruptions and engagements of society and business, at home and abroad, and by the way-side. Such a labour makes no ordinary demand on the faculties and energies of the mind, and they continually call for that preparation of heart, which divine teaching and aid can alone afford.

Indeed, in view of what has been said, every reflecting parent must be constrained to exclaim, "Who is sufficient for these things?" An amiable and intelligent young mother was once visited by her pastor, on her request to see him, for the purpose of a conversation on personal religion. He did not find her, however, evincing any special concern of the usual character, such as distress for sin, apprehension of God's wrath and a desire for his favour. On the contrary, she candidly acknowledged that she was not affected by views of that sort. But she said she desired to be a Christian, that she might thereby be fitted for the right performance of her duties to her children. The burden of the parent's prayer in relation to the unconscious babe, from its earliest existence, should be in the spirit of Manoah's prayer when he desired that the man of God (the angel) might be sent "to teach us what we shall do unto the child," Judges xiii. 8; and we have great encouragements to prayer, when we reflect on the fact, that one of the evident designs of the family constitution was the increase of true religious knowledge and piety. Those who seek grace then for those duties, by which they hope to promote the best interests of their children, are praying, so to speak, in the direction of God's purposes. We are also encouraged by the tender concern which the blessed Saviour manifested for these "little ones" when on earth, and may feel assured that though now raised to his glory he still "suffers" us to bring them to him, in the arms of parental affection and christian faith.

II. The duty of thus presenting our children to God is one of early and constant force. From their birth and even previously to their birth, and on frequent and special occasions, as the recurrence of their birth-days, during seasons of sickness, when leaving home on visits or for school, and at other similar periods; often, in family prayer, in secret prayer, in special prayer, "with and for them," and above all, most solemnly and devotedly, with "strong crying to God and tears," in the sacrament of Baptism, should parents thus dedicate their children to the service and love, and worship and enjoyment of God, the Father, Son, and Holy Spirit.

For a discussion of the authority, nature, obligations, and advantages of infant Baptism, our readers must be referred to the numerous able and excellent treatises which are easily accessible. Such a discussion would be here out of place, even did not our limits forbid its introduction. Yet we may offer a few suggestions :

(1.) Christians are intimately connected with Abraham by faith in Christ, and thus heirs of the promise. Gal. iii. 7, 29.

(2.) The promise to Abraham, though including temporal blessings, was specially a promise of spiritual blessings, for Paul calls it the Gospel which was preached to Abraham. Gal. iii. 8.

(3.) Of the covenant by which this promise was given, circumcision was the appointed sign and seal, and not a mere political rite. For it is said that Abraham received it as a seal of the righteousness of faith, Rom. iv. 10 ; that is, as a seal of the covenant. It was a seal of Abraham's accepting the conditions of that covenant, as well as of God's promise, in the covenant.

(4.) But Baptism has come in the place of circumcision. Col. ii. 11, 12. In the Jewish church, circumcision was the initiatory rite, applied to the adults who were converts from heathenism. Ex. xii. 44–49. So is Baptism the initiatory rite of the Christian church, to be applied to all who profess their faith in Christ. The moral meaning of the rites is the same. cf. Rom. ii. 26 ; Col. ii. 11 ; 1 Pet. iii. 21.

(5.) Hence, as Christians are "Abraham's seed," the Church under both dispensations is the same. Rom. xi. 17–24.

(6.) And as children born of Jewish parents were thus entitled to circumcision, as by birth members of the visible church, so children, born of Christian parents, are members of the visible church, and so entitled to Baptism, which is the sign of such membership. Gen. xvii. 14; Acts xvi. 15; Gal. iii. 27.

(7.) The children of one believing parent are entitled to this ordinance, just as Timothy was circumcised because his mother was a Jewess, though his father was a Greek. 1 Cor. vii. 14; Acts xvi. 1–3.

Christian parents, then, should bring their children to Christ in baptism, and thus secure for them those blessings, which are offered to us, in this ordinance. They should impress on their minds the duties they have been thus pledged to perform, and use every means to make this ordinance a means of grace. Larg. Cat., Q. 167.

III. Under the obligations of the baptismal vow and in accordance with the nature of the family constitution, parents are bound to take care of the proper education of their children. We use the word education in its wide sense. It is that process by which we "lead" or "bring out" or train the faculties of body, mind, and heart.* Following an order, suggested by this threefold view of the nature of education, we proceed to mention those duties by the discharge of which parents may hope to secure its greatest benefits to their children. As we shall have occasion in the next chapter to discuss the means by which the education of children may be best conducted, we shall confine our remarks here to the statements and explanation of those duties, and some of

* Educate, from the Latin *Educo,* to lead or bring out.

the motives by which their performance may be enforced.

(1.) The instincts of nature so urgently induce parents to provide for the bodily welfare of their children, that any suggestions on this subject may appear superfluous. And, indeed, in respect to the physical education of very young children, parents, generally, less need admonitions to the performance of duty, than instructions how to perform it properly. Yet even in such cases, mistaken fondness may set aside the conviction of reason so far, as not only to involve wrong doing, but also to occasion a dereliction of duty.

Physical education consists in a proper training of those functions of the body, by which a healthy, vigorous growth is secured. In respect to children of good natural constitutions, the duty of the parent is to be exercised, chiefly in acts of prevention and restraint. No systems of artificial gymnastics can supply the place of that bodily exercise, to which nature prompts the child. The parent is called on to restrain the indulgence of appetite, prevent needless exposure, excessive exertion, and the engagement in sports, which may endanger health or limbs. He must adopt appropriate means to secure the healthy action of the skin and digestive organs, the full development of the muscles, and the early formation, or rather continuance of those habits of activity and vigorous motion, to which a child of sound constitution is naturally disposed. It is all important, as children become the subjects of mental training, that parents use the most careful precaution against that excessive occupation of the mind, which depresses the animal spirits and weakens the body, by depriving it of suitable exercise. Even granting that the precocious development of the mental faculties is intrinsically desirable, the result is purchased at a ruinous cost, when the health and vigour of the body are sacrificed in its accomplishment. We cannot too earnestly urge on the conscience of parents and especially mothers, the duty of the most assiduous attention to the bodily health of their daughters. Custom, fashion, the perverted preferences of society for what are misnamed "accomplishments" of female education, over substantial and valuable acquisitions of useful knowledge and a sound intellectual discipline, are altogether tending to sap the physical constitutions of large classes of our population. The frail, sickly, nervous, dyspeptic, and often spinally deformed girls, who annually leave our fashionable female academies and private schools, conducted in residences of luxurious indulgence, present a poor promise of mothers for a healthy, vigorous race of sons and daughters. Nor are we without reasonable apprehensions, that posterity will have equal cause to reproach our age for neglecting the rearing of strong and well developed men. We do not desire the training of pugilists, prize-fighters, and rope-dancers; but feeble, sickly, half-grown graduates of universities and colleges, will have made a poor compensation to the nation, by all their learning, for its loss of sound bone and muscle in them and their descendants. Nor, indeed, will mental and moral soundness long survive the depreciation of bodily constitutions. Parents then, not only for their own happiness, and the happiness and well-being of their offspring, but also for the promotion of the prosperity of the nation, and the interests of true religion, are urged to the duty of wisely providing for the physical education of their children.

(2.) Parents are bound to secure to their children the best mental improvement, which their own circumstances and the natural capacity of the child will allow. It has ever been a distinction of our church, that she has carefully promoted the intellectual as well as moral culture of the people. The obligations she imposes on parents in her baptismal service, if complied with, would secure for all her baptized children, the fundamental element of all mental education, and the key to all knowledge, the art of reading. The majority of parents can personally comply with so much of this part of parental duty as requires this instruction. And we remark, in passing, that, ordinarily, such personal compliance is the most efficient, for, in most cases, children who learn to read under parental teaching, make the best readers. But, whatever amount of instruction may be imparted and by whatever agency, parents should bear in mind, that instruction is only a part of even mental education. They must also cultivate in their children a taste for reading and the acquisition of useful knowledge, train their memories to be retentive, quicken their powers of perception, cultivate their imagination, and as the reasoning faculty begins to unfold its nature, aid its proper development. Of course this duty must be modified by the circumstances of parents, as to ability, leisure, or pecuniary means for employing the agencies of others. So also the varied capacities of children, considerations of health, or peculiarities of natural endowments, of inclination, and taste, suggest questions as to specific duties, the discussion of which is neither important in this place, nor allowed by our limits. Still we feel free to say, that much culpable neglect of this important part of parental duty has arisen from the popular prejudice, that an education, conducted beyond instruction in the elementary branches, unfits the subject for the duties of plain life. There may be some just grounds for such an opinion, were the mind cultivated to the exclusion of the culture of the body. But the right training of the body is not only consistent with the culture of the mind, but it is an important auxiliary. Whatever be the future occupation for which the child is destined, the highest degree of mental improvement which can be secured, will, so far from hindering success in any lawful pursuit of life, tend to prepare him for the more efficient prosecution of his purposes. It is true, that mental, so far from superseding the necessity of moral education, is alone generally unproductive of moral benefit. Still ignorance is no more the mother of righteousness than of devotion. The ignorant are, by no means, exempted from the temptations of vice.

Those parents act wisely who so highly appreciate their duty in this matter, that they readily make sacrifices of property to procure, for their children, the best available privileges of mental education. It can easily be shown, that on the score of economy, no better investment of money can be made for a child, than that expended for such a purpose.

(3.) We are informed that one of the offices of the preparatory mission of John the Baptist, was " to turn the hearts of the fathers to their children." Luke i. 17. This somewhat obscure passage, it has been plausibly suggested, teaches that John was appointed to lead the degenerate Jewish people back to the wholesome but neglected customs of their ancestors, (Ps. lxxviii. 3–8,) who were strictly enjoined to instruct their children in the facts and principles of revealed religion. Deut. xi. 18. It must be acknowledged, that some confirmation of this view is found in the adaptation of such a service to the leading purpose of John's mission, "to make ready a people prepared for the Lord." A reformation of families in this duty of religious teaching, would be a reformation of the nation, and one peculiarly important to John's object, in that the people would thus be led to a more careful study of those Scriptures, which testified of Christ. So also would "the disobedient" be turned to the "wisdom of the just," or true piety.

But whether this view be adopted or not, the Scriptures most fully enforce the duty of parents to "bring up" or educate their children "in (or by) the nurture and admonition of the Lord." Eph. vi. 4. The approved example of Abraham, (Gen. xviii. 19,) the explicit directions of Moses, (Deut. xi. 19; xxxi. 13; Ex. x. 2, 13, 14, 15,) and the pious purpose expressed by the Psalmist, (Ps. lxxviii. 3–8,) clearly unfold to us the Divine will as to this duty, under the Old Testament dispensation. Nor was the religious training confined to instruction. The book of Proverbs is replete with admonitions to parents not only to instruct their children, but also to discipline them. The sad example of Eli, "whose sons made themselves vile, and he restrained them not, (1 Sam. iii. 13,) is evidently presented, as a warning against the neglect of parental discipline; for it appears that he most faithfully and tenderly admonished his wicked sons, (1 Sam. ii. 23–25,) but "he restrained them not." To instructions and admonitions to the performance of this duty, the Scriptures add encouragements. "Train up a child in the way he should go, and when he is old he will not depart from it." Prov. xxii. 6. This promise is confirmed by the many instances of piety produced by parental faithfulness which are presented in Scripture, such as Isaac, Jacob, Joseph, Moses, Samuel, David, Solomon, Josiah, and Timothy, as well as by the Scriptural view of the nature of the family constitution, which God has sanctified to the work of extending true piety in the world.

It is a most marvellous and lamentable inconsistency that parents, in the face of Scripture precept, example, admonition, and promise, so often neglect the religious care of their children, even when they have been dedicated to God in Baptism. This neglect is the more glaring, when combined with a proper care for the bodily and mental improvement of children, and especially, when the consequence of this. The best physicians may be sought to detect and repulse the lurking approaches of disease, or repair its ravages, or aid in the right development of the bodily organs. Costly journeys are taken to secure access to genial airs and healing fountains. Even expensive tailors and dress makers are hired to adorn the body. The best schools are sought, often with no regard to religious character, to provide instruction in letters. But with all this the soul may be left to perish for lack of knowledge. Well may we say to such parents, "These ought ye to have done, and not to leave the other undone."

In the light of the Scriptures, a religious education consists in the careful inculcation of the truths of revelation, according to the child's capacity to receive them, and a judicious system of discipline, by which the child may be most effectually restrained from the indulgence of evil propensities, and be led to the formation of religious habits. Parents must not only restrain them from evil, but avoid any conduct themselves which may, directly or indirectly, exert a bad influence. They are warned not to "provoke their children to wrath," (Eph. vi. 4,) which is often done by undue severity, the capricious exercise of authority, partiality, or other injustice. They must avoid sowing the seeds of evil in their hearts, as they would imbuing their bodily constitutions with poison. The indulgence of any sinful habit or the expression of sinful emotions, as anger, jealousy, hatred, revenge, and the like, in the presence of children, are thus forbidden. Let them especially beware of ever deceiving their children. They thus set an example of falsehood, and weaken that confidence which is one of the brightest and strongest links that bind children to parents. They must train them to revere and study the Scriptures, and although, till the heart shall have been truly renewed by God's Spirit, they will not render a Christian obedience to God's law, still they may be trained to the great moral virtues of honesty, fair dealing, tenderness, gentleness, justice, and humanity. They may be led to form habits of daily prayer, reading the Scriptures, and reverence for the Sabbath and the sanctuary. As these are important means, by which they may be brought under the operation of religious truth, and not practices to be substituted for a religious life, the parent must, most earnestly and importunately, seek the Divine blessing, by which alone he can expect to realize the ultimate design of his performance of duty, the saving conversion of his children to God. Parents are urged to this duty, not only by the considerations which are connected with its nature, and that of the family constitution, but also by a regard for the welfare of their families, the interests of society, and the everlasting salvation of their children. For the principles of Christian faith underlie those moral principles, which sustain peace and order in the family, promote the interchange of kind offices, restrain and moderate the ebullitions of evil passions, and encourage and strengthen right affections and habits. It is obvious that the virtues which are nourished in the family, will be those illustrated in society. The customs, confidence, and courtesies of our ordinary intercourse, the laws which regulate our relations, and the sanctions which sustain those laws, have all thus grown up under the fostering influences of true piety.

Even a regard to a wise economy of our resources, admonishes us to train our children on religious principles. Youth needs amusement and relaxation, and those which are consistent with true piety, are far cheaper than those which vicious propensities demand. Many is the drunken or debauched son, or the frivolous pleasure-loving daughter, who expends far more in the pursuit of forbidden enjoyment, than all the religious privileges of a family cost. But that which should most excite our sluggish souls to a prayerful performance of this duty, is the consideration of the spiritual interests of children. If they die during infancy, we entertain a pleasing confidence of their everlasting happiness, as a part of Christ's purchased possession, and belonging to the kingdom of God. But should they remain, after reaching the period of accountability, unreconciled to God, there is no guaranty, merely in virtue of their birth of Christian parents, their baptism, membership in the visible church, and title to its instructions and prayers, that their hearts will be renewed. It is only by the blessing of God on all the means which ought to be used, that such a result can be expected; and surely a neglect by parents of those which it is their special duty to employ, must greatly weaken any expectation of their children's salvation which they might be disposed to entertain. That God may and does convert the children of parents thus negligent, is true, but his promise is to Christian parents who perform their duties and to *their* seed.

Among all forms of human sorrow, what more excites our pity, than that of parents, mourning over the wreck of all their fond anticipations, in the hopeless profligacy of a son, or the "living death" of a beloved daughter! What so grates on a parental ear as the words of an ungrateful child! And over what grave are to be found so few, and such dim rays of comfort, as over that of youth, dying from disease, the fruit of early formed, unchecked, and indelibly fixed vicious principles! If we would deliver our children and ourselves from such mournful calamities, let us diligently engage in the sacred duty of training them for God!

IV. We have thus far spoken of parental duties as they pertain to both parents. But it is generally true, that owing to the father's engagements, the performance of some of the most important devolves chiefly on the mother. This at once displays the admirable wisdom of God, and greatly enhances her responsibilities.

Moralists, poets, and philosophers have vied with each other, in celebrating the relation and moral influence of woman. She sings the lullaby at our cradles; catches with joy the first rays of intelligence, which beam from our infant eyes; first pours into our minds the wonders of redeeming love; teaches our trembling steps the ways of life; watches our wandering feet, when they stray from God; soothes our broken hearts with the sweet promises of the gospel, and sustains our drooping spirits by the sure words of hope. In doubt she is our counsellor, in adversity our comforter, and when fortune fails and friends desert us, she inspires us with her own confidence and hope, by the assurance that we have her faithful love. As the last scenes of life approach, she watches our dying pillow, with moistened cheek whispers to our departing souls the consolations of her faith, and not till the last glimpse of flickering life has died on our deadened eye-balls, and she has closed their lids, does this first, last, best friend surrender her trust.

Those qualities which distinguish wife, sister, and daughter, concentrate in the mother, with the addition of the instincts which belong to the relation, wherever existing. It is to her, thus fitted to instruct ignorance, sustain feebleness, awaken energy and alleviate distress, that God, in the wise economy of the family constitution, has assigned the most important post of moral agency. As the child draws from her breasts the first nourishment of the frail body, so from the fountains of her love, it derives the first food of the immortal soul. As by her sensitive ear, its cry of distress is most quickly discerned, so to her tender heart its appeals for help are never made in vain. On her falls the duty of giving the first direction to its capacities for right, and imposing the first restraints on its tendencies to wrong. The hold on the child, acquired by these intimate relations to its early life, is retained through all the years of its subjection to parental authority, unless severed by some sinful cause. By this means, as her children grow up around her, she becomes the sympathizing friend, teacher, and counsellor, and through life remains united to them, by a bond of the tenderest ties and most enduring power.

Corresponding to her position in respect to her children, are her special duties. To her care, must be assigned the formation of their manners, their decent appearance in society, and the regulation of their household duties. It is her part to see that they attend to their daily studies, prepare their lessons for Sabbath-school and the catechetical class, are in their places at family worship, and in the house of God. Besides the duties to her daughters, which she shares with her husband, she is especially appointed their adviser in their most delicate and important interests both of body and soul. She must watch, with her unerring instincts, against the formation of habits pernicious to health; direct them in dress; instruct them in the minutiæ of household duties, which, however intrinsically unimportant in detail, yet in the aggregate, are material contributions to family comfort and order; carefully prescribe and control their demeanour to the other sex, and guide them to understand and illustrate the true dignity of woman.

V. Parental duties do not cease with the period of the children's subjection as members of the family circle. Parents will still impart to their children judicious counsel and aid them in their lawful pursuits, by the lessons of their own experience.

According to their ability they ought to render suitable pecuniary aid to their children when they settle in life. As to the amount, proportion to their prospective inheritance, and similar topics, no specific suggestions are required. It is perhaps best on this subject, to act on the general principle of avoiding equally one extreme position, according to which, children should be left to their own resources, and the other, according to which, they should be at once supplied with all to which they might ever expect to lay claim.

Every head of a family should have a will always ready. Let such be drawn up in proper legal mode, and accurately and clearly prescribe the disposition of property. Especially let testators avoid all appearance of partiality, or undue discrimination among their children. Thus heart-burnings, litigations, and alienations of near relatives will be avoided. Ordinarily, men had best be the executors of their own donations to benevolent objects, so as to leave their children no ground to feel that their rights had been invaded for charitable purposes.

Finally, let parents avoid improper interference between their children, and their "children's children." By advice, they may render their children great aid in their new and untried position; and if residents of the same house, be eminently useful as teachers and guides of their young grand-children. But they should beware of presuming on their position, and not forget that their children are also parents. The only grand-parent whose special relation to children seems to have claimed the notice of the Spirit of inspiration, was Lois. 2 Tim. i. 5. Let her example encourage, stimulate, and direct others to secure like celebrity, as not only the possessor of faith, but the successful teacher of its principles to the third generation.

When grand-parents are entrusted with the management of the orphaned children of their sons or daughters, they are placed under the responsibilities of parents, and should feel the additional obligations, which arise from the circumstances of peculiar tenderness, with which their relation becomes invested. So also older brothers or sisters, or other relatives, on whom parental duties to orphan children have devolved, are placed in a position, to the duties of which the remarks now offered must apply.

SEC. IV. *The Responsibilities and Duties of Children.*

According to the nature of the family constitution, the filial relation is one of dependence and obligation. Hence arises the great law which prescribes the duties of this relation. This is the law of filial obedience. It is a law of nature, the obligation of which is recognized, to a greater or less extent, in all states of society. This law, as well as all others which affect man's moral interests and relations, is more clearly taught in the Holy Scriptures. God enounced it as one of those "ten words," (Ex. xxxiv. 28, *margin*,) or laws of immutable and universal obligation, which he declared amidst the fire and smoke of Sinai. "Honour thy father and thy mother, that thy days may be long upon the land, which the Lord thy God giveth thee." Ex. xx. 12. Our Saviour re-enacted this law, when he vindicated it from the false interpretations of the Pharisees, (Mark vii. 10–13,) who by their traditions had virtually set aside its authority; and he condescended at once to explain and illustrate its teaching, by being "subject" during childhood and youth, to his earthly parents. Luke ii. 57. The apostles introduce it among their precepts for the instruction of mankind in the relative duties of life, expound its nature, and enforce its obligations. Paul interprets "honour" used in the fifth commandment, by "obey," thus indicating that obedience is the fundamental principle of the commandment, and will produce that reverential regard, which is denoted by the more general term: "Children, obey your parents in all things, for this is well pleasing unto the Lord." Col. iii. 20. Elsewhere, (Eph. vi. 1–3,) he appends to this precept, given in substantially the same terms, a quotation of the commandment in the words of the preceptive portion, with a modification of those which express the appended promise.

1. According to these inspired declarations, we learn that this obedience is required "in all things." This very comprehensive phrase teaches how the law of obedience is the foundation of all the prescriptions of filial

duties. The only limitation to which this requisition is liable, is expressed by the words "in the Lord; for this is right," or, as the same idea is elsewhere (Col. iii. 20) expressed, "for this is well pleasing unto the Lord." In these words, we have a farther definition of the nature of filial obedience, as well as a limitation on its extent. We are thus taught that it must be rendered, like that of the wife, on Christian principle, with a proper sense of accountability to the Lord Jesus Christ. As parents are thus inhibited from requiring their children to do any thing which violates the obligations of Christian duty, so children are taught, that the performance of their duties to parents, is not suspended on the personal character of the parent, or their own feeling of dependence or obligation, or any other contingency, but on the immutable authority of God. In the combination of these defining phrases we are therefore taught, that the obedience of children, as that on Christian principle, must be prompt, implicit, and cheerful; not that sullen, reluctant submission of a forced will, but the ready, good-natured compliance of an affectionate heart; and that it is due to all the lawful commands of parents. It is true, that by reason of sin, the performance of the duties of this filial, as of other relations, may be much embarrassed. The misconduct, and even tyranny of godless parents, produces cases of great hardship. But in no case are children absolved from their allegiance to parents, except when the commands of the latter are contrary to the commands of God; and even then, a course of Christian forbearance and patience may do more to effect relief, than that of positive rebellion. No reconstruction of society can provide a better agent for the protection and care and training of children than the parent. The family is "the earliest, cheapest, safest, mightiest institution," to secure to children the instruction and aid they need. The evils contemplated then must be endured. This is better than to jeopard the good, which is provided by the law of filial obedience, by vain efforts to avoid its abuses.

To return—the obligation of this law of obedience is enforced by the promise annexed. Paul's introduction of the promise and the language in which he gives it, are thus interpreted by a recent, able expositor of the passage.* "This is the prime commandment; the first in importance, among those relating to our social duties, and it has the specific promise annexed: It shall be well with thee." Whether this view be adopted, or that which, by "first," designates simply the order of this commandment, in the second table of the decalogue, it is very evident, that the annexation of the "promise," is an important feature in the statement here presented. Generalizing the words, as given in the decalogue by Moses, which had a special reference to the residence of the Jews in Palestine, Paul makes them applicable to obedient children every where. Among the Jews, the rebellious son was condemned to condign punishment by the hands of the civil power. Deut. xxi. 18–21. Solomon's counsels to children, (Prov. i. 8; iv. 1–12; vi. 20–22,) and his frequent warnings against filial wickedness, (Prov. xvii. 21, 25; xix. 26; xx. 20; xxx. 17,) show that even under the Old Testament dispensation, the

* Dr. Hodge on Ephesians, vi. 1–3.

specific form of the promise was an indication of the general blessing of "prosperity and happiness" of which "long life" is so often used as the expressive symbol. Ps. lxi. 6; xci. 16. Prov. iii. 2. Such is the principle of the Divine government now, as the observation and experience of men attest, though liable, as other general principles, to such exceptions as the arrangements of God's providence may demand; and its operation is exemplified as to individuals, "as far as it shall serve for God's glory and their own good." S. Cat. Q. 66.

To all the regulations of parents respecting dress, manners, play-mates, hours of rising and retiring, food, recreations, labour, the use of medicine, or other means of recovery from sickness, or relief from pain; and whatever else may affect their own welfare and happiness, or the order and comfort of the household, children must submit. Even the most trivial matters to which allusion has been made, may have very important relations, and, at all events, it is by disobedience in such, that habits of disobedience are gradually formed, which may ultimately undermine authority. There are, doubtless, many short graves in our church-yards, whose tenants might have been alive, but for their resistance to parental authority in regard to food or medicine, or some similar matter.

2. When young persons approach that period of life, which has been called the age of discretion, or the boundary between childhood and youth, or have actually become capable of the proper exercise of reason, many occasions arise, to test the power of the great principle of filial obedience. Then the influence of motives to

obedience, drawn from the fitness of the case, the right of parents to command, or filial affection, may be invoked, to secure a proper regard to parental authority; but underlying all these, without whose support they may fail of effect, is this law of God: "Obey your parents in the Lord." Hence, throughout the period of youth, children should continue, most implicitly, to revere the authority of their parents. Thus, (1.) they should select their associates and their books, which may be the most dangerous or most profitable companions, according to the direction of their parents. (2.) Let them be cautious in spending the money with which they may be entrusted, in any way contrary to parental wishes, expressed or implied; and to secure a check on any tendency to depart from this rule, let them keep a careful account of expenditures, and submit it to the inspection of their parents. A regard to these suggestions is enforced by the lamentable evils, which often ensue by their neglect, in the formation of vicious principles and habits, under the influence of "evil communications," whether of persons or of books, and the rise and growth of dispositions to concealment as well as to extravagance.

(3.) Children should have no secrets from their parents. They should early and constantly cultivate the most unreserved intercourse with these, their natural guardians, and best friends; repose on them their entire confidence, consult them on all occasions of doubt and trial, and meet with frankness and candour all their advances to encourage such confidence. Many a youth has commenced a course of fatal defection from truth and duty, by making confidants of indiscreet or evil-minded persons, and concealing his sentiments and plans from his kind and judicious parents.

(4.) Youth are often solicited to engage in what some term "innocent amusements," such as dancing-parties, or games of chance, or perhaps to attend the theatre or race-ground. A consent to such solicitations, "only once," it is urged, "can do no harm." But such a consent does not "honour" parents, whose disapprobation is well known, whether any perceptible evil be inflicted on the disobedient child or not, in a particular case. It is well known, that, even granting an innocent or indifferent character to pertain to a particular act of dancing, or gaming, or attending the theatre, it paves the way for another, and but few repetitions are necessary to induce a taste for amusements of this kind, which proves a snare of souls, and leads to vices, that often drown men in perdition. The best security for youth is, therefore, not in their reasoning but in strict obedience to parents.

(5.) Youth and even children who have advanced in their education, beyond the elementary stage, are often tempted to question the propriety of pursuing some particular branch of study, deemed important by their parents or teachers, to whom parents have confided the conduct of that part of their education. It is needless to remark that mistakes are often made by the most judicious parents and teachers in such matters. But we cannot discuss exceptions. Ordinarily, they are the best judges. At all events, the pupil is not the proper judge. He can know nothing of the absolute or relative value of Latin, Greek, or mathematics. Let him sedulously aim to comply with parental wishes. Sometimes parents, whose means do not permit them to give their children a liberal education, endeavour to have them trained to some honest and useful occupation, by which they may earn a livelihood, and such should cheerfully adopt the course thus indicated. In all such cases, disobedience or a wilful neglect of the proffered advantages of a preparation for the duties of life, almost inevitably leads to lamentable results. In either case, a disobedient child, if not able fully to have his way, will perhaps so conduct himself as to disappoint the parent. Neglect of due diligence in study or labour, resulting in ignorance for knowledge and inefficiency for capacity, lays the foundation of greater evils. Perhaps the teacher or master mechanic, worn out by incorrigible conduct, dismisses the boy in such disgrace, that all similar advantages with others are forfeited. Unfit for the sphere of life to which they had been destined, and by lost time and the habits of idleness formed, prevented from seeking any other, such youth often become the grief of parents, useless drones, and successful candidates for graduation in the school of vice. Or if, with some partial acquirements, they undertake the duties of a calling, failure and disappointment from incompetency add strength to those habits of idleness which have been partially contracted in their efforts to elude or resist parental authority. For though discouraged from labour, Satan, who "ever finds some mischief still for idle hands to do," encourages them to vice and dissipation. Idleness and vicious indulgences, alternately causes and effects, soon bring their inglorious career to a close, in the appropriate graves of obscurity and infamy. The Sabbath-breaker, the thief, the highwayman, the pick-pocket, and the murderer have often dated their disgrace and misery from the first act of disobedience. Numerous youth of both sexes, and all grades of society, may be found, in all parts of our land, who most painfully illustrate the evils of filial disobedience. How many half educated or half-trained young persons are there, who idly doze away their mornings in the sluggard's slumbers, spend their days in lounging, tattling, and gossipping, and their evenings in frivolous gaieties, or the perusal of pernicious books; while their parents laboriously toil for the support of their useless, and worse than ungrateful, sons and daughters!

(6.) Let not children despise the moral restraints and religious instruction of their parents. Even should they not appreciate their value, they ought to submit cheerfully to the use of all those means, by which parents may endeavour to train them for heaven. Let them beware of yielding to the sophistical suggestions of their own hearts, or of wicked men, that no benefit will arise from instructions which they neither appreciate nor desire, and restraints which are unsuitable to the season of youth. Some such suggestions will be discussed in a succeeding chapter. Chapter vi. It should be enough for children to feel that their parents desire, and also know, what will best promote their welfare; and though they may not appreciate their commands, let them *obey*.

3. When youth approach the period of adult life, although they may not be subject to the same methods of parental control as at earlier periods, they should still

be governed by the spirit of the great law of filial obedience. Should they have grown up disobedient, they will rarely reform, except by the intervention of God's grace. But if they have been obedient children, under right culture, they will more readily continue to yield submission to parental authority, when the convictions of reason and the dictates of enlightened conscience shall have come to sustain its requisitions, and especially, when a right home culture has been attended by the promised blessing of a Divine renewal. Ps. lxxviii. 5–7.

(1.) As those requisitions assume more and more the character of advice, so the grounds of conformity will become more and more those of reverential regard. Such youth, amidst all the glowing hopes of that ardent period, will still entertain moderate estimates of their own powers, and defer to the guidance of parents. When these, by their education or position, have entitled themselves to such deference, this respect for their authority is obviously as easy as it is amiable. But it often happens, in our rapidly progressive land, that parents rear families of children to the enjoyment of far greater privileges than they ever possessed, especially as to the advantages of education. Now young persons, whose fathers and mothers are thus intellectually their inferiors, will often be tempted to slight their advice, even on subjects within the limits of their knowledge and capacities. This is a violation of the great law of reverence due to parents. Sensible persons will not demand more respect than that to which they are entitled, and children, properly reared, will be ready to defer to the opinions which claim that deference, as well because they are those of parents as for their correctness.

(2.) On no subjects are youth more liable to violate the spirit of the Divine command, which we are considering, than on those of marriage and its antecedents. Many, otherwise dutiful and respectful to parents, become so far the dupes of the false views which often prevail, that they studiously avoid all consultation with them, on the propriety of their preferences, or the methods to be adopted for securing success in their matrimonial projects. Some proceed so far, in this palpable disregard of parental control, as to evade those laws which inhibit marriage when under age, except on the permission of parents, by escaping, like culprits, beyond the jurisdiction of the State of their residence.

Now with all reasonable concessions for the force of mutual attachments, and with the admission that parents may sometimes be unreasonable in their objections, we must contend, that these palliations of this very popular kind of disrespect and disobedience, are not a justification. The error begins in a want of that confidence which children should cultivate. It is aggravated by a false view of the nature of marriage, of which we have before spoken. Passion may mislead the judgment, but true love implies its exercise. Young persons should abstain from associating with those, a union with whom would incur parental displeasure. These remarks apply particularly to females, inasmuch as few males marry under legal age. In so far, however, as they commit themselves, while under age, to a connection disapproved of by parents, they violate parental and State law in effect, though the connection be not formed till they are legally permitted to act independently. Both parties incur great risk. A young woman should be guarded how she subjects herself to one who has not learned to obey; and a young man, how he takes to his bosom one who begins a life of professed obedience in one relation, by an act of distressing and insulting disobedience in another. It has been often observed that such marriages, with few exceptions, prove unhappy; thus sustaining the old adage, that an undutiful son or daughter does not make a good husband or wife.

(3.) Indeed, in whatever relates to a settlement in life, as the choice of a profession, the location for business, and the methods of prosecuting it, dutiful children will yield readily to the advice of those, of whose good will they can have no suspicion, even should the propriety of some of their suggestions be questioned. As they become engaged in the active pursuits of life, let them never permit the most engrossing occupations of their callings, to prevent them from showing to their parents marks of respect, by visiting and cheering them amidst the infirmities of age, and aiding them, if poor, by contributions to their support. How touchingly beautiful are these eminent examples of filial piety, afforded in the lives of Joseph and David! The former, amidst all his glory and royal dignities in Egypt was mindful of his aged father, and brought him to be "nourished in the best of the land," (Gen. xlvii. 12,) and the latter, when a hunted fugitive, before the envenomed rage of a powerful and vicious rival, found the means to provide a secure refuge for his father and mother, till he could know what God would do for him. 1 Sam. xxii. 3. And with what tenderness, did the blessed Jesus, in the last moments of his expiring agonies, when "he saw his mother and the disciple standing by whom he loved," say "unto his mother, Woman, behold thy son," and "to the disciple, Behold thy mother!" John xix. 26, 27. Children should show a filial regard for parents, after their death, by scrupulously executing their wills. Even should there have been made an injudicious distribution of property, let no reflection be cast on the honour of the parent, by a refusal to abide his decisions. Rather let children submit to injustice, if they innocently may do so, than tarnish the reputation of a parent, by the expression of a suspicion of his fairness.

Children who have families of their own will derive great aid to their efforts in training their children, by thus conducting themselves in regard to their own parents. Their example will deeply impress their sons and daughters with feelings of respect and veneration for them; and thus, while rendering a tribute of duty and affection to those who are passing away, they will be preparing those who come after, to entertain and evince like sentiments towards themselves.

To their teachers, as far as they occupy the place and perform the duties of parents, children owe the same kind of obedience and honour, during their temporary relation. They should behold in the teacher, only a substituted parent, and nothing would more tend to smooth the paths of teachers and pupils, than the cultivation of a reverential regard for the former, in the minds of the latter.

Indeed, it would be easy to show that the spirit of the Bible law ought to influence the young in their demeanor to all their seniors in age and superiors in authority. "Thou shalt rise up before the hoary head, and honour the face of the old man," (Lev. xix. 32,) is the inspired precept. A proper regard to the opinions and feelings of older men will exercise a healthy conservative influence on the opinions of the young, and thus on that of society, in which they must soon be actors. Could we see this great law of subordination fully recognized in th^ conduct of those who are now young, we might well rejoice in the future of our country. When in virtues, as well as vigour, "our sons are as plants grown up in their youth," and "our daughters as corner-stones, polished after the similitude of a palace," we may well exclaim, "Happy is that people that is in such a case." Ps. cxliv. 12–15. That such may be our case, let us earnestly endeavour to inculcate on all children, in families and in secular and Sabbath-schools, the principles and duties of the Divine law of obedience.

OF BROTHERS AND SISTERS.

The Scriptures have not included the relation of brothers and sisters, among those whose duties are made the subject of special instruction. Yet the common relation they sustain to common parents, and the influence of their conduct to each other, not only on the peace and order of the house, but on all the means of parental government, will justify a few suggestions on their relative duties.

The parental admonitions to the cultivation of kindness, gentleness, forbearance, meekness, tenderness, forgiveness, self-denial, generosity, and benevolence in their intercourse, if duly heeded, will ensure the performance of their mutual duties. Brothers especially owe to sisters the most marked politeness, that which springs from the heart-felt desire to make others happy. They should cultivate the habit of showing them the deference due to their sex, yielding to them the first places in the domestic circle, and endeavouring to promote their comfort and happiness. Boys are often known to lavish such attentions on other girls, while neglectful of their sisters. However proper the one course, the other is wrong. Let sisters, on the other hand, not be exacting in demands on their brothers. They may make them full amends for their deference, by contributing to their entertainment while in doors. They will thus materially aid in cultivating in their hearts a love of home, and few boys are in danger from temptations, who truly love home. They may greatly aid in checking the natural tendency of boys to rudeness, soften their manners, and, at the same time, greatly encourage them to diligence in duty, manliness, and uprightness. There is a mighty power for good in the influence of a gentle, loving sister on a brother. The older should aid parents in instructing and training the younger, not by domineering or usurping authority over them, but by the kind and gentle deeds of sympathy, by aiding them in their lessons, encouraging them to effort, preparing means for their innocent amusement, and, above all, by setting an example of the virtues which they ought to imitate.

The Scriptures have used these terms of relationship,

to express that of the members of Christ's church, thus not only sanctifying them, but also intimating the tender and endearing intimacy of the relation: and our Lord has been pleased to reveal himself to his people as their "elder Brother." Christians are exhorted to "love as brethren." Let brothers and sisters love as Christians, be faithful in their common and their mutual duties, and thus enhance the value and the loveliness of the family constitution.

SEC. V. *The responsibilities and duties of Masters and Servants.*

The necessities of every civilized community demand a class of labourers who sustain the position of inferiors to those whom they serve.

This state of society has occasioned several topics of inquiry, belonging properly to the science of political economy, which we are not here called to discuss. They are topics, on which the sacred writers have forborne to instruct us, as they have also on similar subjects touching the various forms of civil government. But they have very distinctly recognized the relation of master and servant, and fully taught the nature and obligations of the duties of both parties. Indeed, no relation of this life has received more attention from the writers of the New Testament. Our Saviour uses its tenor to illustrate the relation of himself and his disciples, incidentally recognizing the superiority of the master and the subjection of the servant. Luke xvii. 7–9; xxii. 27. John xiii. 16. Paul, in several of his Epistles, (1 Cor. vii. 20–22. Eph. vi. 5–9. Col. iii. 22. 1 Tim. vi. 1–6. Tit. ii. 9–10. Philemon 10–17,) and Peter, (1 Pet. ii. 18–20,) have fully explained the nature, and earnestly urged the obligation of the duties of both parties. These full and frequent inspired teachings on this subject were peculiarly pertinent, because, during the apostolic age and wherever Christian churches were formed, there existed a form of servitude, peculiarly severe and oppressive on servants, and which exposed masters to unusual temptations to an abuse of power. Both masters and servants were among the converts to Christianity; and the sacred writers, without discussing any questions touching the expediency or necessity of the relation, but treating it as a fact in the constitution of society, apply the principles of the gospel in defining and enforcing the duties to which it gives rise.

Of several passages already referred to, we quote the following, as presenting a connected exposition as well as an excellent and comprehensive summary of the inspired teachings.

"Servants, be obedient to them that are your masters, according to the flesh, with fear and trembling, in singleness of your heart, as unto Christ. Not with eye-service as men-pleasers, but as the servants of Christ, doing the will of God from the heart; with good will doing service, as unto the Lord, and not unto men; knowing that whatsoever good thing any man doeth, the same shall he receive of the Lord, whether he be bond or free. And ye masters, do the same things unto them, forbearing threatening; knowing that your Master is in heaven; neither is there respect of persons with him." Eph. vi. 5–9.

In this and the parallel passage in Colossians, the duties of servants appear to be more specially and fully expounded than those of masters. We observe also that both in the Epistles to Timothy, and that to Titus, and in the Epistle of Peter, they are fully presented, while no special address is made to masters. This peculiarity of the apostolical teaching on this relation is partly explained by the obvious consideration, that servants are liable to the influence of peculiarly strong temptations to neglect of duty, and are, at the same time, exposed to suffer under a tyrannical abuse of authority, by which, in this sinful world, at all times their lot has been signalized. Hence they need the more emphatic admonitions to duty, and the more pointed exhortations to persevere in well doing, amidst all the untoward circumstances of their situation. But if we consider the phrase, "Ye masters, do the same things unto them," we shall have reason for regarding masters as more fully exhorted, than the brief portion expressly addressed to them might seem to imply. All that regard for Christian principle, which is urged on servants for the regulation of their conduct, thus becomes as fully applicable to masters. Indeed, as the duties are correlative, we may infer that whatever be the conduct to which servants are exhorted ought to meet corresponding conduct on the part of masters; so that if the former are to render an "earnest, conscientious, and religious service," the latter must exercise an earnest, conscientious, and religious government." Eadie on Eph. vi. 9.

I. The word "master," is the translation of a Greek word, κυριος, meaning *lord*, owner or possessor. The more common term, Δεσποτης, to designate one sustaining this relation, used in other places, (1 Tim. vi. 1. 1 Pet. ii. 18,) is indicative of absolute control or despotic authority.

1. This authority however, is limited by the phrase "according to the flesh," which distinguishes the master on earth, from the Master in heaven. His control only extends to that which is external. His right to the labour of the servant does not imply a right to control his conscience. The soul of the servant is free. The master may not abridge his religious privileges, to which he is entitled according to his station in life, nor can he justly hinder his performance of religious duties. The master's right does not include a right to abuse or injure his person by cruelty, or to use him for other purposes than those which are implied in the right to fruits of his reasonable labour.

The master's authority is farther limited by the phrase, "do the same things to them," as already suggested; this means that the master as well as the servant must subject his conduct to the control of Christian motives and principles. He must rule as subject "to the Lord," as "fearing God," and as "doing the will of God from the heart." As the servants of "believing masters" must not "despise them, because they are brethren," so masters of believing servants must treat those servants as brethren, though brethren in an inferior station of life.

Though the power of the master is despotic, the despotism is not that of an irresponsible ruler, but that of the family constitution, as prescribed by God and having its foundation in love. The master must love his servant, not as an equal, but as a servant, and accordingly treat him with all that consideration of his welfare, which the relation subsisting permits and requires.

2. The general principle of such treatment is thus

laid down: "Masters, give unto your servants that which is just and equal." Col. iv. 1. The servant, in authority, station, and other circumstances of social life, is inferior to the master. But this inferiority does not destroy the social and domestic rights and privileges which belong to him as a human being, in the sphere in which God has been pleased to place him. Such he may forfeit, as others may, by crime, or he may lose them by unavoidable dispensations of Providence; but in no case is such forfeiture a necessary incident of his condition as a servant.* This precept farther inculcates on masters the duty of fairly compensating servants for their labour. Peculiar circumstances connected with the commercial condition, and other interests of particular portions of the country and the world, so vary the value of labour and the cost of living,—and individual interests are necessarily so modified by those of the class to which they belong, that it is impracticable to lay down specific rules for regulating the conduct of masters in the particular, now under consideration. This much, however, may be regarded as a sound exposition of Scripture teaching capable of general application. Masters must avoid taking advantage of the necessitous and dependent

* We are pleased to know, that under the influence of a healthy public sentiment throughout our Southern States, a growing respect for the sanctity of the family union among servants has long existed. In some states, public sentiment alone very generally prevents its needless violation; and in others laws, vigorously enforced, have secured for this class of labourers, as great and often greater exemption from an invasion of their integrity and peace, than exists in those countries where the exigencies of poverty alone produce such consequences.

condition of servants. The provision for their remuneration should secure for them comfortable lodging and clothing, and sufficient wholesome food. This is the average, when helpless children, the infirm, the feeble, and the aged are comprehended with the able efficient labourers, as a class, to which as such they are entitled. In reaching this average we are also to take into view a proper consideration of the burdens and casualties of the service, and the value of the aid which masters give to render the labour of servants more productive. Servants should also be allowed every innocent gratification and suitable recreation, compatible with that steady and mild exercise of the master's authority, which is necessary to promote the welfare and happiness of both parties. Conscientious masters will carefully look after the health of their servants, not only by securing for them when sick all requisite medical aid and nursing, but also by restraining them from habits injurious to health, and providing for them in all seasons of infirmity and helplessness, whether of early life or declining age.

3. Under the obligations of the Scripture precept, "to forbear threatening," masters are bound to a humane and considerate regard for servants. Thus they should not address them in angry and harsh terms, using sneers, gibes, and taunts, or expressing unkind and uncharitable suspicions of their integrity and fidelity. They should not make rigorous exactions of service, but appoint a reasonable task, prevent needless exposures to inclement weather or liability to the necessity for any undue or unreasonable exertion, and give a candid consideration to excuses for delinquencies and imperfections.

Kindness and gentleness may be mingled with firmness in all governments, and punishment of whatever nature is always more efficient when administered with calmness, and under an evident sense of performing, conscientiously, a painful but necessary duty. The obdurate and intractable are thus more readily subdued than by threats and bursts of passion, or sudden and angry inflictions of any kind of punishment. Sympathy, compassion, and protecting care will solace the suffering, make tranquil the slumber, and content the spirit of the humblest servant, while acts of a Christian temper pleasing to God, will produce a blessing to the master himself.

4. The condition of servants, being, for the most part, one of poverty, dependence, and ignorance, they are exposed to many evils through the ill will of others, or their own imprudence and improvidence. Against such it is the duty of masters to fortify them by all proper means. They should warn them against the artifices of those who would take advantage of their peculiar condition, by defrauding them of their rights, in their petty commerce, or by inveigling them into vicious practices, or who would injure their characters or persons by defamation or violence. They should protect females from insult and degradation, and both sexes from undeserved accusations and punishments. They should also endeavour to train them to habits of neatness, care, and economy. Their position tends to render them thoughtless and improvident. They are not only in danger of regarding exemption from labour as the highest happiness, thence indulging in idleness whenever they have an opportunity, but they are peculiarly liable to make foolish outlays of money for present

gratification, regardless of the future. It is one of the frequent incidents of their condition in life, to look forward for provision against the wants of age, to some source out of themselves. Masters, who regard the best interests of those who serve them, will endeavour to overcome these propensities which enure to their ultimate unhappiness.

5. It is the duty of masters to exercise a watchful care over the moral and religious interests of those placed under their control. They should earnestly warn them against the evils of intemperance, and the vices which prevail so often among persons of the labouring classes. They ought to urge all, and require the younger, to use the appointed means for their religious culture. So far as possible, let them personally instruct them, whether by set lessons of some systematic form of religious teaching, or by conversation, in the doctrines and duties of religion; and set them a pious and godly example, impress them with a proper sense of their responsibility to God, and by every possible mode show them that they are equally concerned that their servants should perform their duties to God, as to those who rule over them in this world.

To the faithful performance of the duties now expounded, many incentives may be addressed to masters.

(1.) They should feel urged by a proper consideration of the station and circumstances of those under their control. Servants are relatively poor. Over the poor, the Scriptures teach us, God extends a peculiar care. Benevolence to such is a duty to him, which he will not fail to reward, (Lev. xix. 10. Deut. xv. 11. Ps. xli. 1.

Prov. xiv. 21,) while their oppressors are the objects of his holy indignation. Is. iii. 14, 15 : x. 1, 2. Prov. xxii. 16. Ps. lxxxii. 1–4. Our blessed Lord "became poor" and "took on him the form of a servant." Phil. ii. 7. 2 Cor. viii. 9. He thus honoured poverty, and by his sympathy with the poor and his tender kindness to them, left us an example for our imitation, in the exercise of that pity and gentleness, for which poverty appeals to a Christian heart. There is also a peculiar power in the touching appeal, "Behold, I am thy servant!" which may be considered as addressed to the master, by one who is dependent on his care, whose services have enured to his advantage, who has perhaps watched over his infancy and childhood, ministered to him in sickness, and shared the sorrows of his bereavements and afflictions.

2. The general Christian duty to the ignorant and unenlightened in the truth, which "makes wise to salvation," is specially obligatory on the master. While called to "do good unto all men," as he "has opportunity," (Gal. vi. 10,) he should feel incited to labour for the spiritual benefit of his servants, both by his abundant opportunities and their great need. He has control of their time, and can secure for them privileges which, left to themselves, they would neither ask nor seek. They are ignorant, and by the necessity under which they are placed to be continually engaged in labour, are often deprived of many religious privileges, which others enjoy, even if desiring them. They are credulous, easily misled and exposed to sore trials of principle. Like all other human beings, they will have

some religion. This reflection is specially worthy of attention, when it is borne in mind, that servants exert a great influence on the youth of the family, as nurses and companions of their childhood. Not only therefore, the spiritual well-being of the servants, but the interests of the master, whose prosperity and happiness is connected with their moral character, the principles and conduct of his children, the peace, order, and well-being of the family and of society, conspire in urging on him the duty of providing for them instruction, and training in the truths of revealed religion; the system of faith which alone teaches man how to live well and to die happy—alone fits for the duties of time and the destinies of eternity.

3. Let masters remember that "they have a Master in heaven;" neither is there respect of persons with him. Eph. vi. 9. Before his bar, all must appear, divested of all the authority of earthly relations, and held to a strict account for the "deeds done in the body." Happy will those be, who can there meet servants, eternally blessed by their agency, and present them as crowns of their rejoicing for ever.

II. SERVANTS* are subjected by the apostle to the

* The Greek word Δουλος, translated *servant*, has the more specific sense of *slave*. Such is evinced by its etymology, being a derivation of Δεω to bind, and by its opposition to ελευθερος, free. Eph. vi. 8. 1 Cor. xii. 13. Rev. xiii. 16, &c. The best Lexicons, such as Wahl, (Robinson's translation,) Bretschneider, Passow, Liddel and Scott, and the leading commentators, Poole, Scott, Macknight, Olshausen, Eadie, and Hodge, all sustain this view. Even when used in a figurative sense, the word expresses the idea of stringent obligation or devoted service, as may be seen by its use to denote the relations of Christians to the Saviour. Rom. i. 1. Phil. i. 1. Acts xvi. 17, &c.

same great law of obedience under which children are placed, and the nature and limitations of that obedience are substantially the same. They are exhorted to "do service as unto God and not man," "with fear and trembling," or an anxious solicitude to please him, "in singleness of heart," or sincerely, "as the servants of Christ," (Eph. vi. 5–9,) and "to please their masters well in all things, * * that they may adorn the doctrine of God our Saviour." Tit. ii. 9, 10. Obedience to "their own masters" is a part of the duty they owe to their "Master in heaven;" and yet while due "in all things," the most abject cannot be scripturally required to violate the dictates of an enlightened conscience, since the duty to his "master according to the flesh" is limited as well as defined by his duty to God, to which such a violation would be opposed.

During the apostolic age, and in those countries of which the early Christians were residents, servants were peculiarly liable to those temptations to disobedience and that neglect of duty, which are always incidental to their condition. The instructions and admonitions of the inspired writers are well adapted to such a state of things.

(1.) Servants are exhorted to sincerity and honesty in their deportment. "Singleness of heart" is opposed to all duplicity or hypocrisy, such as those evince, who make an appearance of labour while loitering, or who

---

We prefer in this discussion, and with this explanation, to retain the more general term *servant*, as our Bible translators have done; which denotes the condition of all, whether in bondage or freedom, who are subject to the control of others.

promise readily and perform lazily, or do not perform at all. It is also opposed to "eye-service," which a mere fear of punishment, as only desiring "to please men," to their own advantage, might produce.

(2.) "Not purloining but showing all good fidelity." Tit. ii. 10. Purloining or "keeping back," as the word here used is elsewhere rendered, (Acts v. 2,) is a vice to which some servants are peculiarly addicted, under a false principle of morals, that while honest in their relations to others, they may appropriate to themselves the property of their masters, which may be the fruit of their own labours. Indeed, all the vices forbidden in the eighth commandment are incidental to poverty. Prov. xxx. 9. But the apostle admonishes servants that such conduct is a breach of "good fidelity," which itself is eminently the result of a conscientious Christian obedience. This fidelity also requires that servants avoid wilfully or carelessly destroying, injuring, or wasting their master's property, or permitting others to do so, if it is in their power efficiently to interfere; and as their reasonable appointed labour is part of such property, they are bound to the profitable employment of their time. The vices to which sincerity and fidelity are thus opposed, are those to which all servants are, more or less, inclined. They do not appreciate, if they always rightly comprehend, the connection of interest which may exist between their masters and themselves, and cannot, by any reasoning, either specious or sound, be induced properly to apprehend the duty of care, diligence, and honesty in a service, which they regard as enuring only to another's benefit. It is only on the principle of Christian obedience, that faithfulness in these particulars can be efficiently inculcated.

(3.) Servants are exhorted to "count their own masters worthy of all honour," and to avoid despising them, especially if "believers." 1 Tim. vi. 1, 2. Though as opposed by "doing them service," the word, "honour," may here mean obedience; yet as already explained, it may be taken in the wider sense of reverence, or that mingled fear and love, which secures obedience as well to the known or implied wishes of the master, as to his explicit commands. It implies respect for the person of the master, and a polite and deferential demeanour towards him. It is opposed to "answering again," (Tit. ii. 9,) and to all that sullen, ill-concealed reluctance, which marks an obedience only compulsory in its cause, and selfish in its ends.

(4.) Patience and submission under merited chastisement, is urged by the apostle, (1 Pet. ii. 18–20,) when he reminds servants, that the only "glory" of "being buffeted," is in being "buffeted wrongfully." Those who do wrong and suffer for it, cannot prefer a claim to be the victims of persecution for conscience toward God. Hence, obedience is urged, not only to the "gentle," who may not be disposed to adopt harsh measures to enforce it, but also to the "froward," who will be ready to use them.

We are interested to notice how the sacred writers have uniformly enforced every suggestion of duty by an allusion to Christian obligation. The fear of God and relation to the Lord Jesus Christ, (1 Cor. iii. 22–24,) at once indicate the disposition and the motive to duty.

A regard for the name and doctrine of God, (1 Tim. vi. 1, 2. Tit. ii. 9,) and a desire to honour him in the persons of his believing children, are adduced as incentives to Christian honesty and humility; and the rewards of the inheritance, to be meted out in the great day according to what every man doeth, whether "he be bond or free," (Eph. vi. 8. Col. iii. 24,) are held forth to stimulate the servant to zeal, diligence, and a conscientious performance of the most trying, and often the most thankless offices which men are ever called on to render for the benefit of others. Let not the humblest Christian servant be discouraged. Though poor and despised of men, let him remember that the Lord of glory honoured poverty and servitude by becoming poor, and taking "on him the form of a servant," and he too was "despised of men." Let him then seek to walk in the steps of Christ, and by patient continuance in well-doing put to silence the ignorance of foolish men. His toils and hardships may wear down his vigour, and the ingratitude and wickedness of the cruel, drink up his spirits; but he is not degraded. The great Master has reached down the hand of his mercy, spoken peace to his heart, made him a freed man of Christ Jesus, and thus given him hopes which survive all earth's sorrows, a freedom which no shackles can diminish, and a nobility which no earthly potentate can confer. Nor is it to be forgotten, that even in this world, such secure the confidence, respect, and love of their masters, and of all wise and good men. Let those who have "believing masters," aim rightly to improve the spiritual advantages they possess.

Were masters and servants imbued with the true spirit

of the gospel, no part of the family constitution would more strikingly illustrate the beneficent influences of Christian principle, because, in no part does our depraved human nature find more frequent or influential occasions for the manifestation of its worst passions, and the greater the obstacles, the more glorious the achievement. Let masters earnestly address themselves to their duties, and servants with humility and docility accept the instructions of the word of God, and then the evils which a rash philanthropy would remove, at the risk of inducing far worse, would be gradually subdued before the purifying and ennobling power of Christian principle. All earthly relations will soon terminate. Masters and servants who may have lived on earth in the performance of their respective duties, under the influence of Christian motives, will soon rejoice together, as heirs of the common grace of a common Father, when the toils and temptations, and the anxieties and griefs of time shall have been forgotten, amidst the ever growing glories of the redeemed servants of Christ in heaven.

CHAPTER III.

THE BEST MEANS TO SECURE THE ENDS DESIGNED BY THE FAMILY CONSTITUTION.

If the several members of a household perform their duties, as perfectly as is consistent with that moral infirmity which pertains to man's best services, we are persuaded that the family will be a nursery of sound morality, useful knowledge, and true piety. In such a household, love, peace, and order will reign; and, "so far as it shall be for God's glory," and the good of its members, health and plenty will abound. Those inmates of the house who are of mature age, will be the most reliable elements of a prosperous state and an efficient church; and those growing up under their influence, will be prepared to take their places, and transmit to others, after them, the benefits of this wisely ordained institution for promoting man's present and future welfare.

That the family constitution is not always productive of such results is, alas! too true. But such failures are not ascribable to a defect in that constitution. They are due, either to ignorance or neglect of the means by which, in the providence of God, the duties essential to success may be properly performed. In speaking of the nature of the family constitution and the duties of parents on whom its character and efficiency mainly depend, we have had frequent occasion for adverting to the essential connection between the proper government and instruction of children, and the successful operation of the family constitution. The means, therefore, by which children are rightly educated, are those of leading importance to secure the ends designed by this organization.

SEC. I. *Family Government.*

A well ordered family government is not only a most valuable means for the purpose in view, but sustains such an intimate relation to all other means, that without it, their efficiency is greatly impaired. The memorably disastrous failure of Eli in his parental duties, to which we have before referred, was owing to an inefficient government. We learn that he instructed and warned his sons, but "he restrained them not." We are warranted in supposing, that his sons had been carefully instructed in the truths of revealed religion, but their neglect of duty and indulgence of sinful passions had made them vile, and, with all their advantages of knowledge and privilege of position, finally wrought their ruin. There may be still found but too many illustrations of Eli's faults. Such give countenance to the frequent allegation that the children of the pious derive no benefit from a religious education. But whenever such an allegation is made in respect to any special case, let the inquiry be also made, whether there has not been a repetition of Eli's mournful fault. There may be a right government connected with a defective course of teaching, so far as such an incongruity is practicable, and then also will there be deplorable results. But this fault occurs less frequently.

1. As obedience is the fundamental principle of all filial duties, so the requisition of obedience is the prime element in the exercise of parental authority. At the earliest practicable period of a child's life, a training to prompt, implicit obedience should begin. This period is earlier than many suppose. Even the infant, yet hanging on the mother's breast, may be taught to submit to her will. If the habit of obedience be fixed in early childhood, the task of the parent in governing, and that of the child in obeying, will daily become easier. But the longer parents neglect laying this foundation, the greater will be the difficulty of establishing authority and conducting that government, which depends on its establishment.

Said the mother of John and Charles Wesley, "The first step to form the mind of a child, is to *conquer* its will. When once subdued, then many indulgences can be safely granted."

Said the guilty Webster, when about to die for the fatal blow he dealt poor Parkman—not in malice but in rage—"In early childhood, mine was a quick and off-handed temper, *which was never subdued.* I was a petted and indulged child, and all this is the end of it." Restraints are necessary for the young.

Commands and prohibitions should not be too much multiplied, lest by forgetfulness or a weariness in securing compliance with many minute requisitions, the inattention of parents produce carelessness in children. To avoid a similar evil, parents should beware of hasty or

10*

capricious orders, now sternly requiring a duty, or prohibiting an indulgence, and then, with no sound reason for the change, readily remitting all exercise of authority. It is of great importance, that parents embrace opportunities of giving practical lessons on the connection between obedience and happiness. They may, without descending to a coaxing process, impress the minds of children with this truth, by requiring their obedience in things, which call for little or no self-denial, but to which they are not specially predisposed, and then gradually advancing in the nature of their demands, till their children begin to feel, that, at whatever present inconvenience to themselves, obedience to their parents ultimately secures their own happiness. It will greatly aid in this work, if parents will always be careful to impress the minds of children with the conviction that they are their best friends, and most earnestly desire their happiness. They should condescend to take part in promoting their innocent enjoyments, by affording them proper means of amusement. It is one thing to gratify all the whims and caprices of children, and another to gratify what is reasonable; injudicious parents often act as if they regarded the amusements of their children as utterly unworthy of their notice, and some seem to delight in needlessly abridging them, interfering with their plays by unseasonable and often unreasonable requisitions to some annoying and, it may be, useless engagement. In both cases, there is danger that children will associate obedience and unhappiness, and will be tempted to more diligence in devising excuses than in performing duty. Those, on the other hand, who find parents always ready to grant proper gratifications, and studious to promote their welfare, even in requiring the performance of duty, will be led to the exercise of that confidence in their parents' wise regard for their interests, which, as they increase in years, will become the efficient cause of a prompt, cheerful, and implicit obedience. We hardly need add, that unlimited indulgence is utterly inconsistent with any training to obedience.

Acts of disobedience should never pass unnoticed. In every test to which the child is subjected, the parent should be clearly the conqueror. By this course, such tests will become more and more infrequent. Above all, let parents, at the earliest period of the child's dawning intelligence, impress its mind with the higher obligation to obey God, and endeavour to fix the conviction, that the obedience to the parent is subordinate to that due to a heavenly Father. Children are capable of appreciating the force of such an obligation in very early life, and when deeply fixed, it becomes a surer principle of filial obedience, than any consideration growing out of the parental relation or the obligations of gratitude; while it is also a foundation for a system of religious teaching. Indeed all those systems of securing obedience by hiring children, by means of some indulgence or gratification of appetite, or extravagant rewards in money or other valuables, are of doubtful propriety, in view of the evils which the rewards often entail on them, and ought to be utterly discountenanced, as nnavailable to any right training to the duty of a true filial obedience.

2. Kindred in nature, and one of the first fruits of a training to obedience, is a training of children to habits

of self-denial. Its earliest lessons are gained by obeying, for every act of obedience which requires of the child the repression of his own desires, or a disappointment in his own plans, is also an act of self-denial. The restriction of appetite, denial of coveted toys, the prohibition from some kinds of sport, and the requisition to some conflicting duty, will be suggestive of the nature of such training. But here too there should be caution, lest by enforcing self-denial, without securing by its exercise some benefit to themselves or others, children should be led to look on all such requisitions as rather the acts of an arbitrary tyranny, than of desire for their good. When, however, they perceive clearly a manifestation of such a desire, and find that self-denial, though often a painful duty, may become a pleasing one, in view of the proposed results, they will become ready for the practice of this important element, in a wise training for the stern realities of life.

3. The judicious use of rewards and punishments is a subject of great difficulty in all plans for the government of the young. We cannot consent, with the Scriptures as our authoritative guide, to give place for a moment to the suggestion, that children are to be controlled by mere moral suasion. It is true, that as they develop the reasoning faculties, they should be treated as rational beings. It will indeed be a healthful exercise, to require them, on suitable occasions, to practise the simpler processes of reasoning, and accustom themselves to rely on their own judgments in matters of less moment. But passion and inclination, even after reason asserts her

claim to be heard, are often too impetuous to be restrained by her yet feeble authority.

God has sanctioned an appeal to the hope of rewards and the fear of punishment, as motives of conduct; and the proper exercise of reason is not so much in teaching what is right, as in directing us to a proper appreciation of the rewards of well-doing, and the penalties of evil-doing. Now, at any age, but especially when very young, children are almost daily called to submit to regulations, the propriety of which they cannot understand. It would be vain to hope, that by mere explanation and persuasion, the ignorant child can be induced to receive the nauseating drug, or be restrained from imprudent indulgence in improper food. The rewards which good conduct produces, as legitimate fruits, may be supplemented by promises of special favours as additional encouragements to obedience. But such should not be offered as a hire or as the sole incentives. As the good which follows well-doing is contrasted with the evil which follows ill-doing, so these promised favours may be offsets of special threatenings. Parents should always scrupulously fulfil such promises of reward. Care should, meanwhile, be used to train children to regard obedience as *right*, and that it should not be rendered merely to obtain a reward or avoid an evil. Rewards and punishments are means, not ends, of virtue.

To secure the good effects of punishments they should be most faithfully inflicted. It is more important that they be certain than severe. Indeed the severity is a matter of discretion, in which parents must consider the age, temper, temptations, and advantages of the child, and the nature and alleviations or aggravations of the offence. There is a large class of punishments to which none should ever resort: such as shutting up children in dark closets, starving them to submission, wounding their feelings by gibes and sneers, or abuse, and striking them with the hand. The Bible is a book of eminent practical wisdom. It makes no mention of these modes of punishment. But it frequently urges the importance of a discreet use of the "rod of correction," by which the "foolishness" or wickedness "bound in the heart of a child" may be driven out. Prov. xxii. 15. "The rod and reproof give wisdom," and "he that spareth his rod hateth his son." Prov. xxiii. 14; xiii. 24. The use of the rod does not imply a needless severity. Indeed, the wisdom of this "Divine ordinance," as it has been called, is manifested in the selection of an instrument, by which the measure of severity may be judiciously modified. Objections to its use on the ground of the degradation which it imposes, with the pain inflicted, will apply equally to all species of punishment. In fact, the degradation is rather in the ill-desert, than the punishment which is incurred. Many parents make the sad but candid confession, that they cannot punish, except when in an angry mood! This is much to be deplored. Such punishment as anger inflicts, is seldom judicious in time, degree, or method. The use of any instrument is then liable to be excessive. Haste and passion may involve the parent in that great guilt of punishing the innocent, and a resort to blows with the hand may be followed by painful consequences for life. Nothing more weakens discipline than for parents to make a false charge, and inflict undeserved punishment. The child's sense of justice will be wounded, and the sting will long remain. Proper and deserved punishment will fail in producing its appropriate effect, and the parent himself will, perhaps, under the reacting impulses of his feelings, become as unduly lax as he had been unduly rigorous.

Corporal punishment should not be used on slight grounds, nor be frequently called into requisition. We have often thought that it would be well, if some one, as much superior to parents, in size and wisdom, as *they* are to their children, would be appointed to administer to these hasty, passionate disciplinarians some chastisement, similar in degree and method, to those which they visit upon their offspring.

The Apostle directs that parents bring up their children "in the nurture and admonition of the Lord." Eph. vi. 4. By admonition, we understand the whole process of correcting, by words and acts, the faults, or enforcing the duties of children. Now this is such as the Lord directs. It is a Christian duty. It should be pervaded with Christian principle, and administered in a Christian manner, and for Christian purposes. The best conducted school we ever knew was that of a gentleman, who always preceded the chastisement of a pupil by a season of prayer "for him and with him." This deliberate and solemn procedure, savoured, as it would be, with parental tenderness and affection, would effect more to reclaim the erring and stimulate the sluggish, than scores of hasty, angry, and severe beatings with the rod of correction.

4. Not only ought the age, temper, and general char-

acter of the child affect the degree of corporal punishment, but should influence the parent in every process of discipline. A word of reproof or even a look, will often effect for one, what the rod will be requisite to produce in the conduct of another. Quick and irascible, but easily subdued tempers need more frequent, though milder methods of discipline, than those of a more impassive but stubborn nature. On one, encouragement is more efficacious than disapprobation. The frown which almost breaks the heart of one little culprit, will be returned, by a more resolute and refractory child, with pouts and insolence. In this connection, we may add, that careful training should be used, to lead all children to act on principle, instead of impulse. For the frequently recurring exigencies of life, which call for prompt decision and energetic effort, it is highly important, that youth should be habituated to act, not on the mere suggestions of a passing emotion, but on the well defined purposes of a clear sense of duty, and a firm determination to do what is right, under all circumstances of hazard and temptation.

5. We add a summary of what we believe useful hints on family government, but on which we cannot enlarge.

Those who govern others should learn to govern their thoughts, temper, words, and actions ; to be slow to speak, and speak slowly.

They should be mild but firm, patient with the faults of those under them ; should sympathize with them in sorrow, be helpers of their joy, and set an example of forbearance, self-denial, and forgiveness.

Parents should never allow their children to be away

from home at night, without knowing where they are, and how employed.

Finally, all the members of a family should be trained to punctuality, promptness, and regularity in business, moderation in enjoyment, and patience in adversity.

SEC. II. *Physical Education.*

We have already had occasion to advert to the importance of physical training, as a part of the education, by which children are fitted for their place in society; and it is fully entitled to our consideration, as one of the means by which the design of the family constitution may be secured.

Such a training is effected as much, or more, by the use of preventives than by any course of art or scheme for bodily exercise. Perhaps more injury has resulted from some of the patented devices of modern times, in respect to the care of children, youth, and adults, than from even a culpable negligence, which has not provided against the evils to which all are exposed.

1. Fresh air and convenient access to a supply of good water are essential requisites for a healthy residence. Those are easily had in rural situations, and no less desirable, though difficult to be obtained, in cities. A family residence ought to be sheltered from bleak winds, and the yard provided with shade trees, whether merely ornamental or productive of fruit. Besides the obvious advantages of such a locality on the score of health, there is a good moral effect produced by the pleasing associations which will gather about such a place. The rooms, especially such as are used for sleeping, should be airy, and well ventilated. By a proper care of all

the offices of a domestic establishment, such as cellars, dairies, kitchens, and stables, the decomposition of substances which engender foul air should be prevented. The neatness of such premises, combined with other circumstances, produces the additional advantage of promoting the personal neatness of the members of a family.

2. Much more of the health as well as comfort of children, and, indeed, of all the inmates of a house, depends on the cook, than on the costliness, variety, and richness of the materials used for food. The quality and soundness of meats and vegetables should be carefully inspected, but the process by which they are prepared for the table is of equal moment. Dyspepsia, derangements of the liver, and a long train of distressing nervous ailments, which seriously affect the state of both mind and heart, may be traced to the use of improper food. True, in many cases the injury results from food too highly seasoned or too much enriched by the aid of unhealthy condiments. Still, bad cooking—especially of bread—is a prolific source of evil. Children are oftener the victims of unhealthy food than adults ; and while it is the duty of parents, as already inculcated, to prevent their indiscreet use of confections and richly prepared food, every care should be used to provide them with a simple and wholesome diet. Many a cross temper has been increased, if not occasioned, by sour, indigestible bread; and sometimes the punishment inflicted on a little child, would be more properly visited on the careless cook, or the yet more careless nurse or mamma. We are well aware that all the attention which is desirable, cannot be

given, by many families, to these and similar sanatory regulations. Still the poorest in rural places can secure neatness, good cooking, and fresh air; and even in crowded cities, with but few exceptions, all who have homes, could effect far more than many such do, were they to divert some of their expenditure for useless and injurious indulgences, to the valuable purposes suggested in our remarks.

3. The natural disposition of children to take food frequently, though in small quantities at a time, which some consider a species of amusement, ought to be properly encouraged. They should have a taste for a healthy, nourishing diet cultivated, and not be permitted to use painted candies, richly seasoned cakes, and stimulating drinks, to lay the foundation for lives of pain and premature death.

4. Children should be encouraged to follow the dictates of nature, by being permitted great freedom of out-door exercise. Let their bodies be duly protected by comfortably fitting clothing, avoiding too much wrapping, which will induce undue tenderness, but equally shunning the other extreme of incautiously exposing their yet tender frames, by the effort to "harden" them,—a process which has often hardened the little victims of quackery into corpses. The soiling of clothes or even of the skin is a small matter compared with the advantages of constitutions early invigorated. A free use of clean water will easily repair the damage to the body, and is a cheaper and healthier operation than the use of medicine to repair an enfeebled system. Still children should be trained to cultivate true personal neatness, and to

avoid slovenliness of dress. Neatness and morality are nearly akin.

Let parents accustom children to habits of early rising. Sound refreshing sleep is ordinarily best procured by the use of mattresses,—and in order that children should have enough sleep, they should be required to retire early. They need more than adults. It is highly important that they go to bed in a cheerful humour. The foolish custom of keeping lights in their sleeping apartments, when in health, ought never to be countenanced.

5. That children may have well developed bodies, they ought not to be subjected to early and protracted seasons of confinement in a school-room. Circumstances so vary, that no uniform rule on this subject can be prescribed. Generally, however, the age of eight years is a sufficiently early period, at which to place them under the most moderate restraints of school-rooms. Even then, the hours of recreation should treble those of study. As children grow older, the garden, the farm, riding on horseback, or gunning will afford to boys proper opportunities for exercise, both in useful labour and entertaining recreation; while the cultivation of flowers, walks for the purposes of a practical study of botany, or the lighter services of domestic economy, will contribute to the health of girls. Town life, by its very nature, and much more by the tyranny of fashion, places many restrictions on the physical culture of both sexes. Still by a judicious use of such facilities as may be enjoyed by most residents in town, much healthier faces might be seen among the children of our cities.

6. With all our care, children will sicken. They

should be early trained to submit promptly to the use of all the usual methods of treating diseases to which they are specially liable. Though the remark may appear needlessly minute, it is a suggestion of great importance, that they ought to be taught at an early period, to show their tongues and throats. Many a child has been the victim of its own ignorant obstinacy and parental neglect, simply by hindering the physician from a satisfactory examination of these organs. They should be led to regard the doctor as a friend: and hence should not be threatened with him as one who will subject them to pain. Let them learn that medicine, though bitter, is useful, and be trained to proper habits of attention to the healthy condition of their organs of digestion. By watching the earliest appearances of disease, and using simple and appropriate remedies, protracted and painful maladies, permanently seated ailments or early death, are often prevented. Parents should however be cautious, lest by the frequent use of violent remedies, or the injudicious administration of medicine, they foster, instead of preventing or healing disease. Both for adults and children, nature is a good physician, and the aid of doctors is oftener most valuable, when their knowledge is employed to inform us that no medicine is needed.

SEC. III. *Mental education.*

The intellectual improvement of the members of a family conduces to the attainment of the purposes of its constitution. The degree to which mental culture should be carried must, of course, be determined by considerations, which it is foreign to our purpose to introduce. The circumstances of each family and of the several members of each, must exert a controlling influence in the matter. It is enough for us to offer a few general suggestions on the nature of this culture, and the methods by which in all ordinary cases it may be best secured.

1. Though a knowledge of letters is of material aid in all processes of mental improvement, it is not essential. Very young children, before being subjected to a course of instruction in books, may be taught many valuable facts, and trained to habits of observation and reflection. The natural inquisitiveness of childhood should be encouraged by gratification on all topics of useful knowledge, which may be objects of their curiosity, and the explanation of which they can apprehend. It has been often said, that during the first five years of life, we learn far more than at any subsequent period. It does not follow, however, that such learning will always be either useful in itself, or contribute to a useful, mental, and moral progress in subsequent life.

2. Hence, while the process of a mental education should begin with the earliest dawning of intelligence, great care should be used, then, and during all the years of childhood, to give a right exercise to the faculties of mind as they are developed. There is a great temptation to fond parents, to make their children prodigies. Often the memory of mere words is so cultivated, to the neglect of the reflecting powers, that, even in after life, the subject of such a training continues sadly negligent in the use of such powers. A mechanical or drawling method of reading, acquired in childhood, may often be detected in the pulpit or at the bar; and a defective pronunciation or habits of incorrect spelling, sometimes follow men,

from the nursery and school-room, through life. The art of reading is the key to knowledge. But in order to its greatest utility, children should be so taught to read, that they will love the employment. We seldom find bad readers fond of reading, either to themselves, or to others. Some, from disuse, forget how to read. It is of very great importance then, that children should be trained, in early life, to a good elocution, in which may be comprised correct pronunciation, emphasis, and modulation. For young ladies, good reading is a more valuable accomplishment than any or all of those more costly parts of female education, to which the term has been exclusively applied. Parents, whose own cultivation of mind and leisure enable them to be guides, are, ordinarily, the best teachers of their children in these very elementary, but truly important parts of education. Such and all other, however, can contribute materially to the culture of their children by securing for them the society of the intelligent and well educated, and preventing their association with persons of the opposite character.

3. On the comparative advantages of an education at home or in boarding-schools, on which so much has been said and written, we can only offer a few general remarks. In earlier life, for both sexes, and during all the childhood of girls, no influence can be substituted for that of a home of ordinary virtue and intelligence. But there are large numbers of families, who are prevented by circumstances, which they cannot control, from giving their children a suitable education, unless they send them to boarding-schools. Girls who have been rightly reared

under the parental roof, on passing the period of childhood, may often derive valuable advantages to their mental culture, without detriment to their moral character, by a few years' attendance on well conducted schools, in which, by reason of the numbers collected, a full corps of teachers, and a complete scientific apparatus are provided. Of course, a liberal education of boys can, in very rare cases, be obtained, without the facilities furnished by academies and colleges. We have long felt persuaded, that the objection urged against such institutions, on the score of demoralizing tendencies inseparably connected with their literary advantages, is unfounded. It will be found, on careful examination, that more youth become hopefully pious, while members of our well conducted academies and colleges, than can be found in any other class of young men of similar age.* Let the appropriate work of the family be well done, and, ordinarily, public schools will be public blessings.

4. Both sexes should be educated alike, through the period of childhood. Nor is it a disadvantage, should they, for the same period, be associated together in school. For girls, though not so essential as for boys, a liberal course in the languages and sciences is highly important, so far as it can be conducted, consistently with a training in those parts of domestic life peculiarly pertaining to their sex. But we are reminded that for a large portion of the families in our country, these suggestions are of no practical value. It should, however, be the object of all parents, to provide the best possible intellectual training for their children; and those who

* See Princeton Review.—ART. II., January, 1859.

cannot secure all the desired advantages, and are limited to the elementary process, required by our baptismal service, (Directory, vii. 4,) may so direct the reading and associations of their children, that, as they grow up, they will find in improving and entertaining reading a great security against the temptations to sinful pleasures, will form tastes and habits of thinking which will be the means of self-culture, and will become more capable of appreciating the teachings of the pulpit as well as those of pious parents. From the ranks of such youth, have sprung many of the most eminent, self-educated men in all professions, and they furnish the great mass of intelligent, virtuous citizens for the State, and active members of the household of faith.

SEC. IV. *Religious Education.*

But no measure of intellectual culture, unaided by the sentiments of a true Christian faith, will suffice to secure the most important end designed by the family constitution, the promotion of true piety. The necessity and methods of *moral* and *Christian education*, are presented to our attention by the Apostle's exhortation to parents, to "bring up" their "children, in (or by) the nurture of the Lord." Eph. vi. 4. By the word "nurture," may be understood the whole process of instruction and discipline. This must be such as the Lord prescribes, and the authority of his word must be continually brought to bear on the heart and conscience of the child. He must be presented as the Teacher and Ruler, to whose instructions they must attend and to whose laws they must submit. In a word, the religious instruction by which the great purpose of the family constitution is to be attained, must be thoroughly Christian. It is not that derived from the law and light of nature, the precepts of philosophy or the deductions of science, but that which revealed religion imparts.*

1. The Bible supplies lessons of religious instruction, peculiarly adapted to interest the attention, and impress the hearts of the young. By its brief, but graphic biographies, they are presented with examples of faith in God, the advantages of uprightness, patience in adversity, integrity in temptation, meekness under insult, generosity to enemies, fidelity to friends, kindness to the afflicted, and justice to the oppressed. With these are contrasted examples of the evils of malice, jealousy, envy, avarice, hatred, lust, and revenge, the abuse of power, rebellion against God, persecution of the good, and cruelty to the poor. We are thus invited to imitate the faith and patience of the pious, that we may inherit like blessings to theirs, and warned to escape the misery of those who opposed God's government, by avoiding their iniquitous practices. The lessons of our Saviour's birth, childhood, life, teachings, sufferings, and death, provide the foundation of those doctrines of grace, which make wise to salvation.

Now, these are methods of instruction which suit the ignorant, who always learn best by examples. They may fail to apprehend abstract propositions, which they readily grasp and more easily retain, when presented in the narrative of facts. They are also lessons which meet the ever recurring wants of daily family life. The moral of the biographical sketches of Cain and Abel, Joseph

* See Dr. Hodge on Ephesians, vi. 4.

and his brethren, Pharaoh and Moses, Samuel and Saul, David, Jonathan, Solomon, Josiah, Paul and Timothy, and above all of the blessed Saviour, may be used to repress evil, and encourage right feelings and actions. Thus we see that the Bible presents us the most philosophically correct method of teaching, by adapting its lessons to the young, so that, even before their minds can appreciate its abstract propositions, their hearts will be impressed with the truth which those propositions are meant to impart.

2. To the more practical lessons of the Bible must be added the systematized compends of truth, contained in catechisms. The word *catechism* is of Greek origin, and denotes oral teaching. In Luke i. 4, the clause, "the things wherein thou hast been instructed," might be rendered "the things wherein thou hast been catechized," or orally taught. The reader can also compare (in the Greek) 1 Cor. xiv. 19, and Gal. vi. 6, for similar uses of the verb, κατηχέω, from which this term is derived. In the history of the early church, it has been thought by some, that distinct traces of the existence of a special officer, who performed the functions of a catechist, may be found; at all events, we know that the early Christian pastors performed this work, and during the most prosperous days of the church, we find it occupying the attention of the most zealous and faithful agents in propagating the gospel. All the Reformers, from Wickliffe to Knox, engaged in the preparation of suitable catechisms for the instruction of the children and youth. Our church is much blessed in possessing several of these useful compends. That for young children, itself a full and

faithful summary of Christian doctrine, expressed in simple terms, is an excellent introduction to the Shorter Catechism, a work which can never be superseded, either in regard to the fulness, conciseness, or perspicuity of its teachings. It is a striking testimony to its value, that the Methodist church, which, of all evangelical denominations, is the most strongly opposed to our system of doctrine, has adopted into its own catechism, either literally or substantially, the whole of the answers of this "form of sound words," excepting only those few, that express doctrines to which this excellent body of Christians has ever evinced a decided, and, we may add, strange opposition. The Larger Catechism is a fuller exposition of the truths which form the staple of the Shorter. Youth, carefully instructed by the proper use of these compends, will be well prepared in knowledge, and, by the Divine blessing, also in piety, for the position and work of the true followers of Christ.

3. As children reach the period of youth, the Bible may become the subject of a more minute and extended study. Let them read it, in large portions at a sitting, and form analyses of what they peruse. Commencing with the historical parts, as they increase in powers of comprehension and expression, they may acquire capacity for this useful mode of studying the Epistles. From early life, they should be trained to commit to memory, selections of Scripture, especially of the devotional writings, as the Psalms, and the practical parts of the Epistles, with some of our Lord's discourses, as the Sermon on the Mount, and his last address to his disciples. All should read a portion of Scripture daily, and

adopt some method, such as that of reading three chapters daily, through the secular days of the week in the Old Testament, and five on every Sabbath in the New, by which the whole Bible will be annually perused. Religious biography, expositions of Scripture and of the catechism, and some compend of church history, would constitute a course of useful religious reading.

4. While the truths which make wise to salvation constitute the staple of that instruction, which is comprised in a proper method of moral improvement, there are many topics of common morality and some relating to what may be called the minor morals and good manners, which are by no means unworthy of attention. Parents will find themselves sustained by the authority of God's word, in the lessons of truth, which they inculcate on their children's minds on these subjects. The great law in which our Saviour summed up the Commandments of the second table, "Thou shalt love thy neighbour as thyself," (Matt. xxii. 39,) or, "Whatsoever ye would that men should do to you, do ye even so to them," (Matt. vii. 12,) presents in a few words, the principles of justice, uprightness, honesty, generosity, and kindness. The vaunted polished manners of the ball-rooms and parlours of wealth and rank, and "good society," are mere paintings, and often very imperfect, of that genuine politeness, which originates in a heart of a true Christian sympathy for others. Reverence for age, respect for superiors, courtesy to equals, and kindness to inferiors, are its genuine fruits, and all find illustrations in the inspired Scriptures.

SEC. V. *Infant Baptism.*

Our catechism teaches us that infant baptism is a means of grace, (Larg. Cat., Q. 154, 167,) and although an institution, pertaining more to the church, as such, than the family, yet for obvious reasons, most properly to be regarded as a means of promoting the purposes of the family constitution. The benefits of this ordinance are not restricted to the solemn prayers and exhortations connected with its administration. These are valuable adjuncts, and deserve the serious regard of parents and all baptized children. Those children to whom baptism is administered, on the faith of their parents, are in covenant relation with God, and enjoy a position of greater privilege and responsibility than others. For, to such, by means of parental faith, when properly exercised, there has been specially offered, an "ingrafting into Christ, remission of sins by his blood, regeneration by his Spirit, adoption and resurrection unto everlasting life." (Larg. Cat., Q. 165.) Now, while any Christian parent may and ought to feel the obligations of the parental relation to "bring up" their "children in the nurture and admonition of the Lord," it is but reasonable to suppose that those who have offered them in baptism, with a proper apprehension of their duty and privilege, will specially feel such an obligation. If they have exercised the faith called for by the tenor of the covenant of grace, God has been pleased, on his part, to offer to their children as to them, the blessings of that covenant. Such children then, as they reach years of discretion, though, as other descendants of Adam, "aliens from the commonwealth of Israel," are specially encouraged and invited to return to their allegiance. God, in offering these blessings, and thus urging them to accept his offers, provides, in connection with the ordinance of baptism, suitable means for securing their acceptance. The prayers of parents, of the church, and the pastor, and the labours of the latter for their conversion, will be more direct and frequent. They are also brought into a position more accessible to his labours; and when their relation as members of the visible church by birth, under pledges to perform their part of the covenant of grace, in the exercise of faith, repentance, and new obedience, is properly impressed on their minds, we may reasonably hope, this "means of grace" will become truly "effectual for their salvation."

SEC. VI. *The Sabbath and the Sanctuary.*

The preaching of the Gospel and the proper observance of the Christian Sabbath, are properly to be regarded as valuable means for securing the benefits contemplated in the constitution of the family. These means are not only of utility to children, but to all the members of the household. The sacred quiet and rest of the Sabbath, the exemption from the ordinary duties of life, and the opportunity for spending seasons of special prayer, religious meditation and reading, and praising God for his mercy and love, are peculiarly grateful to the Christian heart. Parents have then peculiarly favourable opportunities for religious conversation and prayer with their children. Fathers, who are hurried by the pressing engagements of the week, and mothers, careful and troubled about much serving in domestic occupations, are then at leisure to call to mind their defects in duty, to encourage and help each other in acts of penitence and faith, and endeavours after new obedience, and to engage in the instruction of those placed under them. Did the Sabbath afford man no other blessings, than the means which it furnishes for promoting the religious welfare of families, it would be well entitled to be called a day "made for man." The best Christians are liable to the influences of the engrossing cares and pleasures of life; and this day is most eminently adapted to break the power of the world over our affections, and as well by its appointed duties, as its appointed rest from other duties, to call our thoughts to heavenly things. All its holy hours, except those spent in the public worship of God, should be so employed, as to promote the spiritual welfare of all the members of the family. An agreeable variety of duty may be imposed on younger children so that they may not be unduly wearied. The afternoon especially, according to the useful custom of our ecclesiastical ancestors, ought to be religiously set apart for the instruction of children and servants. The older children may be employed to a judicious extent, in this duty, much to their own profit. Our Directory for worship concisely and yet fully instructs us in the proper use of this important means; and we refer our readers to its excellent suggestions, as supplying any omissions in these cursory hints. Directory for Worship, ch. I.

The public preaching of the Gospel is God's appointed means "of convincing and converting sinners, and building them up in holiness and comfort, through faith unto salvation." It is much to be lamented, that so many families, in our highly favoured land, are, in a great measure, deprived of this means, or enjoy it but rarely; and that others are dependent to a great extent, for the instructions of the pulpit, on those who cannot preach in an edifying manner, or who occupy the hours of God's holy time, in ill-natured, puerile, controversial harangues, or in fanatical ravings on topics unconnected with the glorious grace of the Gospel. Those however, who enjoy the stated ministrations of intelligent and pious men, will find in such, instructions suited to the case of all the members of the family. Not only may all these be taught the way of salvation through Christ Jesus, but each may be reminded of his special duties, instructed how to meet the trials and temptations which beset his path, and admonished, warned, encouraged, and cheered in the ways of true godliness, so that while aided to be a better member of the family, he may also be a better subject of Christ Jesus.

All the inmates of the household should attend church. If it is necessary that any should be detained at home, a rotation in this duty can be observed. Even very young children should be early trained to go up to the house of God. If too young to receive appreciable benefit by the teachings of the pulpit, they will form habits of respect and reverence for sacred things. The solemn quiet and order of a Christian assembly, the public prayer of adoration, thanksgiving, confession, supplication, and intercession, the notes of cheerful praise, and the exposition and enforcement of the great doctrines of God's word, with the more specially tender solemnities of the sacraments of Baptism and the Lord's supper, are well calculated to produce on the wakening minds of children, valuable impressions. Thus if no direct saving knowedge is received, as they grow up their hearts and consciences will be so affected, that their naturally depraved tendencies will be checked, and the way be prepared for the effectual call of the Holy Spirit.

We greatly fear, that there is a tendency in some minds to depreciate the ordinary services of the sanctuary, and to associate hopes for the conversion of souls, only with seasons of unwonted interest and services conducted by extraordinary agencies. While God often visits his church with times of special refreshing, we are yet taught to expect, and encouraged to pray for, the presence of his renewing Spirit, with every dispensation of the gospel of his grace. Though frail, self-deceiving men are liable to the seductions of Satan, in all circumstances; yet it has been proved, that there are special reasons to watch, with painful interest, the progress and results of some awakenings, to which the term Revival has been attached. Spurious conversions, hasty admissions, and other results equally and more to be deplored, have followed such factitious excitements. The combination of faithful parental teaching, and the ordinary services of the sanctuary will be blessed, and in any particular church, these means will often be attended by seasons of the special power of the Spirit. Let us honour God's institutions and he will honour our labours.

SEC. VI. *Family Worship.*

The discussion of family worship as a means to secure family blessings, is almost entirely superseded by the existence of a popular and valuable treatise on the subject, which has been long before the public.* Still a few hints on this topic in the relation which it bears to our general subject may not be superfluous.

1. On the head of a family who conducts the household devotions, his position as the leader of others, his increasing familiarity with truths, thus twice daily brought to his attention, and his confessions and prayers, must exert a salutary influence. All are liable to grow cold and sluggish in religious affections, forgetful of religious duties, and unmindful of religious privileges. One, who is regular and sincere in family devotion, will be more conscientious and diligent in the closet, and these daily occasions to lead the devotions of others will help to keep alive the fire of his own sacrifice. The performance of this duty will exert a happy effect in checking evil propensities and fostering the good. Those ill tempers which too often arise to mar the affectionate intercourse of husband and wife, or parents and children, will be restrained in his breast, who with wife and children around him, comes to the solemn reading of God's word, to unite in the sweet Psalm of praise, and offer a common prayer to a common God and Father. Surely must this service degenerate into the merest formality, ere he who conducts it, can fail to find all his motives to duty quickened, his pious resolutions confirmed, apprehended obstacles to growth in grace weakened or removed, and every enterprise for the welfare of himself and family sustained by these daily recurring opportunities for coming to the mercy-seat to find mercy and

* Thoughts on Family Worship, by Dr. J. W. Alexander.—*Board of Publication*, 1847.

grace to help in time of need. The head of a family with its cares resting on him, amid the perplexities and annoyances of business, is liable to be led away by the greedy love of gold, the besetting vice of our nature, to forget that he is a husband, father, and master. No means could be devised, better adapted to call him back to a proper sense of his responsibility, than this daily occasion to remember the spiritual wants of those, to whom he occupies such important relations, and whose Christian progress may be materially affected by his performance of his duties, as the priest of his house. Thus he will be incited to diligence in training his family to seek the spiritual blessings, which he invokes for them. He not only becomes a better man, but a better husband, father, and master, and while not less mindful to provide for his own, the blessings of this life, will be more concerned to seek for them the true riches.

If blessed with a pious wife, he will contribute to her advancement in holy living. Her spirits will be refreshed, her anxieties soothed, and her soul strengthened, while he leads her in devotion to the throne of grace. And if she be not pious, this daily service will be a most efficient method, by which to point her to heaven and lead the way.

Of course all that we have adduced as to the advantages of this service to the head of a family finds an application but slightly modified, to the widowed mother, the son, or pious teacher, on whom, in the death or absence of the father, the performance of this service will fall. It has sometimes appeared edifying for a pious wife to conduct family worship, when the husband is unregenerate, or, for any reason, declines performing his duty. The propriety of this course must be decided in each particular case, and we forbear offering any remarks, except to say, that anything like assumption ought to be avoided by the wife, and the husband's full approbation should always be secured. She is not hindered from the more private service of praying with and for her children.

2. Family worship exercises a healthful iufluence on the mere secular and intellectual welfare of the household. Habits of early rising, punctuality, neatness, and order are cultivated, by their stated period of assembling as a family. A day begun in the practice of these minor morals, connected with a season of such solemn interest, will be more probably spent in a proper observance of the regulations for the routine of life, which depend for their efficiency on the existence of such habits. The attendance of children on school, the prompt fulfilment of the engagements of business by adults, and, generally, the right doing of what is to be done, at the right time, are specimens of these incidental temporal benefits which arise from this service. The reading of the Scriptures and the offering of prayer call for intellectual effort on the part of those present, whose attention is given to what is read, and to the sentiments expressed in prayer. The bulk of the poetry, used in songs of praise, is well suited to cultivate the imagination, and improve the literary taste of all who become familiar with its use. Nor should we forget that music forms an important part of education, refining the sensibilities, and training the mind to a susceptibility for all delicate and softening influences.

Children accustomed to sing in family worship, generally become fond of the exercise, and the habit of singing familiar psalms and hymns when alone, thus often induced, becomes not only a valuable and pleasing exercise for the mind, but will preclude the entrance of many evil thoughts, and by association, introduce some most important and valuable reflections.

The widely and justly celebrated intelligence of the Scotch peasantry, is, doubtless due more to their religious training, of which family worship is a most important means, than to any other cause. Other nations possess as generally established, and, perhaps, as well conducted parochial schools, but they lack this added power of home teaching. No Bible reading people can fail to become more enlightened. They will learn to think to more purpose and converse more intelligently, and their moral principles will give vigour and activity to mental habits.

3. The religious influences of family worship on all, but especially on the children, constitute its highest commendation. They are thus led from the earliest period, to feel that God is to be honoured, is the source of every good and perfect gift, and that to know, love, fear, and trust him is the highest privilege and most solemn duty. By this service, the first instructions of lisping infancy and childhood are enforced by daily examples; and the lessons of God's word, sanctioned by the conduct of a revered father, will be more indelibly impressed on the hearts of those who receive them. Let those who choose, sneer at the prejudices of early Christian education. The sophistical reasonings with which

men of no religion, or no right views of true piety, endeavour to sap the wise institutions of our fathers, will be more fully considered hereafter. See Chapter VI. If the so called prejudices are right, let them be imbibed, and the earlier the better. Even the "speechless babe" may be taught by the patient stillness of this sweet sacred hour, to associate God's worship with its first ideas of all that is solemn and separate from earth. To older children, and other members of the family, this daily reading of God's word becomes not only a mental stimulant, by the sublimity of its themes, the perspicuousness of its teachings, and the discriminating power of its reasonings, but also a source of actual increase of knowledge of Divine things. Though, from indifference or incapacity, they may neglect the word of God generally, here are about seven hundred occasions yearly, when they are called to attend to its inspired instructions. To those in whose minds the question of awakening ignorance, "How shall we pray?" has arisen, these daily prayers are an answer. Then the gushings forth, in a father's petitions, of his tender anxieties for the spiritual welfare of his household, will often subdue natures hitherto callous to his admonitions and warnings. Through the day, and in the calm quiet of their midnight hours, the words of sacred writ, read with the simple and affecting tenderness of parental love, or those of earnest, wrestling prayer, which went "not out of feigned lips," will be heard in their souls. Those parents with whom children have bowed in daily prayer, will be associated in the minds of such children, with the solemn and tender scenes of the hours of devotion, and their authority will be strengthened, and one of the strongest of earthly attachments will be made yet stronger, by the bands of religious obligation. Happy those parents who have received their children from God in a second birth, and an everlasting life of holiness. Much do they contribute to secure this result, who pray "with and for them," in morning and evening family worship. On all the members of the family, this precious religious service will cast a hallowing influence. Husbands and wives become more truly one in Christ, parents more diligent and children more obedient, masters more considerate and servants more faithful, brothers more tender and sisters more devoted, who have thus, for years, heard together the words of heavenly truth, lifted together to God common songs of praise and thanksgiving, and sought and found in common, at the throne of the heavenly grace, "mercy and grace," in their times of need.*

In concluding these suggestions on the means by which the ends of the family constitution are to be attained, we must remind our readers that we are to expect the blessing of God, rather on their combined operation, than on the use of any one. The employment of all together constitutes a truly happy home. All the plans of parents should conspire to the production of this sweet representation of Eden's bliss, this efficient source of the best affections of human nature. Were we called on to express in one sentence, the sum of all the counsel we have suggested, both as to parental duty, and the

* For the train of thought pursued in the foregoing suggestions, it is scarcely necessary to say that the writer is much indebted to the work already mentioned.

best means to secure family blessings, and their influences on man, we would say, *Make home happy.* But the work cannot be done with similar brevity. We must assiduously cultivate all the means by which it may be performed. As God in nature effects some of his mightiest wonders by the combinations of many littles, so must we rightly appreciate all agencies and influences, even the least. The rain and the dew moisten the earth by myriads of drops; the coral reefs grow by the silent labours of millions of insects. The trees and earth put on the verdure of spring, by the quiet working of countless agencies in earth and air. So we must, by the "mighty power of littles," in the performance of unnumbered duties of daily life, and the use of unnumbered means comprised under any one of the general topics discussed, endeavour to train our households for the duties of earth, and the more solemn destinies of another world. Let us not be weary in well-doing, but patiently labour in all the paths of duty, and by all the means of success, assured that as we sow, so shall we reap.

SEC. VIII. *The means for the religious improvement of servants.*

Much of what has been said on the methods and influences to be used for the religious training of children is applicable to that of servants. But the peculiar position of large numbers in our Southern States, calls for a separate consideration of the best means to promote their religious welfare. We can, however, only present a few hints, and this is less to be regretted, inasmuch as the admirable essay of Dr. Jones,* on this subject, contains all that need be offered, and presents the results of long experience and observation, by one whose zeal and success in the work of which it treats, give him a right to be heard.

1. On the larger plantations of the South, where the servants form a distinct community, the services of a special chaplain are required, who may, by the usual public preaching of the gospel, and schools for the religious instruction of the young, provide for their entire religious culture, as for that of any other community. Or the servants of several contiguous and smaller estates may be united as one charge, under similar arrangements. Or the pastor of the church, in whose bounds the servants reside, may extend to them such special instructions as he has leisure to give, besides preaching to them, in common with others, in the ordinary Sabbath services. This latter method is most practicable in the great majority of neighbourhoods. It was that employed with eminent success, by the Rev. S. Davies and Dr. J. H. Rice, in Virginia, the fruits of which still exist.

2. Where no chaplaincy exists, pastors have but little opportunity or leisure for giving the special religious instructions which servants need. This must be done, as it was in the primitive church, by catechetical exercises. Masters, or other suitable persons in their families, may perform this service. Owing to the great variety of religious sects, and the general preference for particular churches manifested by the slaves, great embarrassments

---

* "Suggestions on the Religious Instruction of the Negroes."—By the Rev. C. C. Jones, D. D.—*Presbyterian Board of Publication.*

arise in the attempts to impart instruction to adults by this method. While some are indifferent and hostile to religious teaching, just as other sinners and for the same reason, that the carnal mind is enmity to the law of God, many, under the guise of attachment to some other church, refuse to accept the religious teaching of those whom they regard as possessed of no more than a religious theory obtained from books. Hence the most efficient means for the religious improvement of servants is the careful instruction of the young. No prejudices here intervene. By the Scriptures and catechisms they can be taught the truths of religion essential to salvation, as well as others. As such persons are remarkably fond of singing, a selection of some twenty or thirty Psalms and hymns, in which the most important doctrines of experimental piety are embraced, may be made, and they may be induced to commit them to memory. They may also be taught select portions of Scripture in the same manner. According to the wishes of the master, they may be taught to read. The art of reading is not essential to obtaining a knowledge of the saving truths of the gospel. Even in those countries in which all classes of the population have secured to them the benefits of elementary education, it has often appeared, that the engrossing occupations of labour and the customs of recreation have virtually deprived the labouring classes of any practical benefit arising from their advantages. Though taught to read, they forget the art by mere want of practice. So it often happens when slaves are taught. In this matter masters may exercise a wise discretion.

3. A question has arisen, whether masters ought to compel the attendance of all their servants on the public preaching of the Gospel. It is one of great practical difficulty. If answered affirmatively, still the opportunities for such attendance are various, and the question then arises as to the church to be selected, when such servants have different religious predilections among themselves and from that of the master. Compulsion of adults, in matters of religion, is, at least, of doubtful propriety. If the young servants are compelled to wait on regular religious services, as they grow up, much may be expected from the formation of good habits. In view of all the difficulties suggested, we are disposed to say, that those who perform their duty, in carefully instructing the young, and using all moral methods of persuasion, admonition, and encouragement to the older, will ordinarily find that the blessing of God will follow their labours to a greater extent than should they rely on compulsory measures alone for adults. The example of Abraham (Gen. xviii. 19) has been urged as conclusive, in respect to compulsory measures. Not to discuss questions of interpretation, it is enough to say, that the relations of master and servant in Abraham's day, and indeed during the Mosaic dispensation, partook far more of the despotic feature, than now exists. The control of the master was more absolute. The population was homogeneous in religious faith. The whole form of government was more patriarchal, and the institutions of religion were of one kind. We have no hesitation in affirming, that the master should use authority to prevent the use of heathen worship, and should as far as possible, by all his domes-

tic arrangements, not only permit, but encourage his servants to attend some place of public religious worship. But when he shall have performed his part to such servants, while under the age of discretion, and used such means to influence them afterwards, as have been intimated, we think he has fully followed the spirit of Abraham's example.

4. Another question has been suggested. Should masters have the sacrament of Baptism administered to their infant servants? If the children of pious parents, the duty devolves on them. If not, then, as indeed in all cases, the affirmative answer involves many difficulties. The master and servant are subject to other laws, the operation of which may entirely prevent him from carrying out the purposes designed by such an ordinance. Again, for reasons already given, the relation of master and servant now is far from being parallel with that which existed among the Jews; and the dissimilarities bear against the attempt to carry out fully the parallel between the circumcision and baptism of infant servants.

5. Of much more practical importance are those questions relating to the means for promoting moral and religious habits among servants. On such especially as concern the marriage and parental relation, whatever be the laws of men, masters are bound by the laws of God, in the performance of those duties already inculcated, to use all appropriate means for sustaining the integrity of the family union, and thus promoting the moral and religious improvement of servants. Besides those general instructions in the doctrines and duties of our holy religion, which underlie all other means to this end, they may

greatly promote it, by providing suitable accommodations for servants, preventing the occurrence of temptations to conjugal infidelity, sustaining the authority of parents, especially of such as are pious, over their children, and restraining all servants from frequenting places of dissipation and vice. Neatness, order, and comfort in their humble homes will have the same moral effect, which they produce in the homes of others: and their personal habits, as to the use of ardent spirits, will greatly hinder or favour the reception of religious instructions. All the arrangements of the house and farm should be so directed, that servants may have command of as much of Sabbath time for Sabbath duties, as is possible, for any persons occupying the places of menials. Masters should readily surrender to them portions of some other day for such recreation or occupation in their own private interests as may be proper and convenient, that on Sabbath they may be at full liberty to engage in the appropriate duties and privileges of holy time.

In these remarks we have not had in view the condition of hired free servants, because, ordinarily, no special means for their religious instruction are demanded; and yet it may be a question for reflection, by those whom it concerns, whether, especially in our large cities, more interest might not be exhibited, and more direct means well employed, for rescuing a large class of such servants from the influences of a baptized paganism. Meanwhile, household servants of every kind enjoy, in family worship and intercourse with superiors, valuable means for their improvement, which those affording them may make abundantly fruitful of blessing.

These hints have already exceeded our proposed limits. The topic is one of too much interest, to be passed over entirely in this connection, but, at the same time, too extensive in its various bearings for a fuller discussion.

CHAPTER IV.

THE RELATION OF THE FAMILY TO THE CHURCH.

OUR form of government teaches, that "the universal church consists of all those persons, in every nation, together with their children, who make profession of the holy religion of Christ, and of submission to his laws;" (Form of Gov. chap. ii. 2,) and that a particular church consists of the same materials, limited by the circumstances of number and place," voluntarily associated together." (*Ibid.* 4.) According to this definition, the family may be regarded as an integral element of the church. For, even when but one parent is pious, the children are embraced in the covenant, and for this reason the unbelieving parent is "sanctified," or set apart as an agent for the service of God, either as "the guardian of one of his chosen ones," or, as the mother of those, who, by their father's faith, are members of the visible church.*

God was pleased to place a high honour on the family, by depositing within its sacred enclosure the germ of his church. The temporal benefits offered to Abraham and his seed, in the covenant, which God made with him, (Gen. xiii. 14, 15; xv. 7, 18; xvii. 2–22,) were but

* See Dr. Hodge on 1 Corinthians, vii. 14.

types of those richer spiritual blessings, which were provided in that memorable act of Divine condescension and mercy; for not only was Abraham appointed the head and founder of a great nation, destined to be "high above all people in praise, in name, and in honour," (Deut. xxvi. 19,) but he was also chosen to be the "father" of the faithful (Rom. iv. 16) people of God of all ages. He and his household were the called,* or, the church of God. While God was pleased to provide for the increase of the visible church, by that of Abraham's natural descendants, he also indicated that the fulfilment of his promise thus to multiply his seed, was suspended on Abraham's performance of his duty as the head of his family in commanding his children and his household after him, "to keep the way of the Lord." Gen. xviii. 19. Whether then we regard the covenant with Abraham as the fundamental principle of the original constitution of a church in the world, or as only providing for a more definite organization of that "congregation of faithful men," who, since the days of Seth had called on the name of the Lord, it is evident that the church of the New Testament rests on that covenant, and that although the seal has been changed, the blessings provided and offered by God, and accepted by his people, are the same under the Christian as under the patriarchal and Mosaic dispensation.†

The peculiar relation subsisting between the family

* The word 'εκκλησία "church," is derived from the verb, 'εκκαλέω, to call out.

† The third chapter of the Epistle to the Galatians, vs. 7–9, 14–18, 27–29, clearly sustains these positions.

of Abraham and the church no longer exists. Still God, in his word and by his providence, as the considerations, advanced in the foregoing chapters, clearly evince, has continued to honour the family constitution, as an agent for glorifying him by dispensing spiritual blessings to man. This great moral purpose to which it is adapted and for which it was in part designed, (see Chapter II,) is the same as that for which the church was solely instituted. Its agency is more limited than that of the church, and the methods by which that agency is rendered efficient, are subordinate to the divinely appointed means of grace, with the dispensation of which the church has been entrusted. They are also subservient to those means. Thus the family, though not a coördinate, is a coöperative institution with the church of God. This relation has ever been recognized by our church. She contends for it doctrinally in the ordinance of baptism, and practically in the position and duties assigned to the pastor. He is appointed not only to preach in the pulpit, but also to be the chief religious teacher of the child. Pastoral visitation, catechising, admonition, and the careful oversight of the ignorant, as well as the anxious and inquiring members of the family, are made his duties. On the other hand, by means of the family organization, the way is opened for the more faithful and efficient performance of his work. The relation of the family to the church, both as a constituent part of the household of faith, and as an important auxiliary in the work of man's salvation, may be more fully developed by some special considerations.

SEC. I. *The family a means for enlarging the church.*

By means of the family, provision is made for the enlargement of the church. We depreciate none of the benevolent enterprises by which it is proposed to disseminate the gospel in our own destitute regions, or in heathen lands. The church is the depository and propagator of the truth. We may not wait, till, by some ordinary dispensation of providence, Christian families may have settled in such regions, and become the agents of rearing another generation in the knowledge and love of the gospel. We must send the living minister, and by the preaching of the gospel "make ready a people prepared" for appreciating and employing the means by which the family constitution may be made a blessing. Then this agency becomes subservient to that of the church. From Christian families, in a very few years, may spring up other Christian families, in quadruplicate or larger proportions, and these, in their turn, may become sources of still enlarging accessions to the household of faith. Did all Christian parents properly appreciate and perform their duties, it is impossible to form any adequate conception of the rapidity and power, with which Christ's kingdom would advance. Had Abraham's descendants, according to the promise, those related to him through Isaac, persevered in the faith and piety of their ancestor, the Jewish nation and the true church of God would have been identical, and the vast multitudes of those national descendants would themselves have approximated to a fulfilment of the promise to be verified as to his spiritual seed. Gen. xv. 5; xvii. 4–6. Rom. iv. 18. Gal. iii. 7, 8; xiv. 29. Even under the imperfect manner in which parents now meet their responsibilities, we are often called to admire the blessed results, flowing from God's forbearing love and faithfulness to his covenant. The statistics of infant baptisms in our church for any given year, compared with the reported accessions by examination, for some period fifteen or twenty years later, give us good reason to believe, that the bulk of such baptized members become communicants. The increasing population of the country, the numbers added who have been baptized in other communions, or never have been baptized in infancy, and other causes, enter, as disturbing elements, into such calculations. Still we are sustained in the general correctness of the above suggestion, by the fact, that such investigations made in particular churches, give very similar results. We have but recently heard there was a family in one of our city churches, whose members, forty years ago, were easily accommodated in one pew. The descendants of that family now fill fifteen pews. The labours of Rev. Samuel Davies, in Virginia, a century since, were greatly blessed. But as they extended over a large district of a sparsely settled territory, they did not result in the immediate formation of many flourishing churches. Yet many of those families, then isolated, which received the gospel by his occasional ministrations, became the sources of other Christian families, and the centres of Christian influence on their connections by marriage, and on their other neighbours, so that, with the materials thus prepared, many churches have since been formed.

Besides the direct increase of the numbers of Christ's followers produced by the increase in Christian households, such often exercise other agencies in the work of enlarging the kingdom of God on earth. A few Christian families—sometimes only one—settled in a destitute region, may become an encouragement and aid to the efforts of a missionary. Much as we must regret to see once flourishing churches decimated, and almost disorganized by emigration; yet this evil is often more than repaired, when the emigrating families scattering and settling in new portions of the country become the means of founding many other churches, and propagating Christian influences in the places of their new residence. Nor should we forget how a well ordered Christian house becomes a blessing to any neighbourhood, even where a church already exists. The example of Christian parents and well trained children and servants will be felt in other families. Their morning and evening worship ascends to God as acceptable incense, and in answer to their prayers, ungodliness is arrested and truth takes effect on the hearts of others. For "ten's sake" God was ready to hold back from Sodom his impending judgments, and we have no reason to doubt that in our day, his providential government may still be thus conducted.

SEC. II. *The family an aid to the pastor's labours.*

Every Christian family is a small congregation. As already intimated, the pastor has, in such a household, materials properly prepared, to receive his spiritual counsels. The children and servants are prepossessed in favour of him and his message. Religious doctrines are subjects with which they are already somewhat familiar, and they have been taught to regard the great objects for which the pastor labours, as the most important which can engage their attention. They will also be prepared for hearing the word preached, with more profit. One great reason why so much preaching is inefficient, is because so many hearers are ignorant of the first principles of Christian doctrine, and are therefore incapable of appreciating and understanding ordinary gospel ministrations. Many do not apprehend the meaning of some of the most common terms used in theology, or the ideas, which such terms convey to their minds, are so confused and indistinct, that no permanent and profitable impressions are made. Again, the instructions of the pulpit need to be followed up at the fireside. The members of Christian families find the lessons of the church confirmed and impressed on their hearts by the lessons of home, and illustrated in the lives of revered and honoured parents, the examples for their imitation. Their confidence in their pastor will not be weakened by the cavils against his teaching and criticisms on his imperfections, which form the staple of conversation at the Sabbath dinner tables of too many families; but by the commendations of his excellencies and the approbation of his instructions, heard from the lips of their parents, they will be led more highly to revere his person, and more candidly and submissively to receive his counsels.

SEC. III. *The family a nursery of active Church members.*

When persons who have been religiously educated become the subjects of the great change wrought by God's Spirit, they often fail to evince as strong emotions of sorrow or joy, in the exercises of conviction, penitence, and faith, as some others manifest. This may be ascribable to that familiarity with religious truth, which they have gradually attained, and their frequent experience of the ordinary convictions and impressions of the word and Spirit. But their convictions are no less thorough, and their change no less decided. Indeed their familiarity with Scripture truth greatly aids the work of sanctification, and they, generally, engage more decidedly and thoroughly in "living unto righteousness," than some who may have appeared more promising at the beginning of a Christian career. Their development of character, as the disciples of Christ, will be more uniform and consistent. They are less liable to be "tossed to and fro, and carried about by every wind of doctrine," to be misled by new and strange customs, and methods of Christian enterprise of doubtful propriety, or, in short, to be seduced by any of the numerous "novelties" which disturb the peace of the Church and bring reproach on Christ's name. On the contrary, they readily fall into the habits of the Christian life, enter with alacrity on its regular, ordinary duties, and pursue them with persevering diligence and assiduity. They form the bulk of that steady, reliable "Church within the Church," to be found in all congregations, who encourage the pastor, by their presence at the prayer-meeting, and their prompt participation in the exercises of the Bible-class and the labours of the Sabbath-school. They are generally ready for every work of benevolence, and if endowed with wealth, become the liberal benefactors of the institutions of Zion.

When they become parents, they are prepared to assume their new responsibilities. They do not worry their pastor with cavils about infant Baptism. They institute family worship and pursue the whole routine of Christian life, to the pattern of which they have been accustomed from their youth.

It is by no means pretended, that such are the only Christians who are thus reliable, consistent, and uniform in their Christian relations and duties. On the contrary, some of the most eminent servants of God have been taken as "brands plucked from the burning." Our remarks, so far as they imply a comparison, rather relate to classes, than individuals, and exceptions to all such general statements are well known to exist and are cheerfully admitted.

SEC. IV. *The family an aid to the devotional services of the Church.*

It occurs to us, in this connection, to advert to a method, which we make no doubt would ultimately effect a most desirable reform in congregational singing; or rather, in some cases, would be the effectual means of introducing congregational singing where it does not now exist. This most pleasing, solemn, and useful part of divine worship is often sadly neglected. In some of our largest congregations, few, except the choir, join in singing God's praises; and sometimes that body is reduced to a few amateurs in music, whose performances, although distinguished for great scientific and artistic merit, are not calculated to aid, very much, the devotions of God's people. Some ascribe the defects of congregational singing to the use of organs, or other instruments of music, where such have been introduced; and suggest their banishment, as a speedy and effectual method for securing good singing. But the same defect is found to exist in churches, which have most decidedly refused to admit any instrumental music. Hence, in such cases, the choirs are blamed, who, it is said, have usurped to themselves alone the work of praising God, and excluded the people from all participation in singing, by the selection of new or difficult melodies, and such as are not adapted to popular use. In most cases, however, it will be found, that choirs are rather the result, than the cause of defective congregational singing. Other causes have been assigned for the evil, of which all complain, such as the custom of singing without parcelling the lines, the want of good music and teachers, the variety of music books, or the use of books with round notes. Now it is perhaps true, that there are particular instances, in which organs or choirs or both have added nothing to the solemnity of the service and discouraged the singing of a few persons; others, in which choirs, by a gradual assumption of privilege, have almost destroyed congregational singing, and even subjected pastors to the humiliating alternative of conducting the worship of God without singing, or submitting the selection of the words as well as the tunes, to irresponsible and injudicious persons. So also on the ignorant or those too careless to provide books, or too indifferent to learn to sing, the other alleged causes of the evil may have operated. But the cause which most generally prevails, may be stated in very few words: *the people do not love to sing;* while this is so, the destruction of all instruments, the dispersion of all choirs, and the banishment of all books from the pews, will not secure the desired reformation.

This reformation must begin in the family. Let singing be practised in family worship. Children love to sing. If accustomed, from early life, to this use of their voices, they will acquire and cultivate a taste for music and grow up to be singers in the congregation. Nor is the benefit of this home culture limited to its influence on the music of the church. The singing of the same melodies and the same words in church, to which they have been accustomed at home, will form the basis of many sweet and tender associations, which may afterward serve to soften the heart to a susceptibility of the solemn truths and impressions of the public worship of God, even when such may have been long resisted. Indeed, when we consider the evangelical character of our psalms and hymns, it must occur to every reflecting person, that the spiritual benefits of congregational singing are highly important. Many valuable truths are thus most deeply and permanently impressed. The mere reading of good hymns is profitable, and the concord of sweet and solemn sounds is pleasing to the ear and to the taste. Much more valuable is that exercise, which associates, with time honoured and delicious melodies, the more time honoured and inspiriting truths of the Bible. In the want of space to pursue this topic further, we refer our readers to the work already noticed.*

Although, ordinarily, the members and even elders of the church are not expected to take part as leaders in the prayers of the sanctuary, connected with the preach-

* Alexander's Thoughts on Family Worship,—p. 226.

ing of the gospel, yet none, who know the power and value of prayer, can be insensible to the importance of social prayer-meetings. To say nothing of the answer to prayer, promised and vouchsafed by a prayer-hearing God, to those who "agree together" in making known their requests to him, which constitutes the leading motives for Christians thus to "assemble themselves together," we are persuaded, that the influence of such meetings on the devotional feelings and experimental religion of a Christian community, cannot be too highly appreciated. But, alas! how often does the pastor find, that he has but few Aarons and Hurs in his flock! While the church may be crowded on Sabbath morning, often the hour for the prayer-meeting witnesses a most meagre attendance. The female members of the church may be well represented, but of the other sex scarcely a twentieth part are present. We once knew a venerable elder, who was candid enough to confess, that he did not attend prayer-meetings, because, he did not wish to be called on to lead in prayer. In some cases, such meetings are held on a secular day, and at an hour when attendance might interfere with the ordinary pursuits of men of business. Hence habitual absence from the weekly prayer-meeting is often justified by the absentee, on the allegation, that his attendance might greatly incommode himself or others having business relations with him. Surely a weekly meeting in the country cannot produce as much inconvenience, ordinarily, as a daily meeting in the cities, and we have found that such may be well attended, for a long season. But even when the time of meeting is fixed for some hour of the Sabbath, we still find that the attendance is thin. We believe the reason for such neglect of social prayer, generally true, is that even those who have some measure of devotional feeling, are unaccustomed to pray in the presence of others. It seldom occurs that those, who are regular and zealous in family prayer, have any material difficulty as to conducting the prayers of others. It is by the home training in praying with his family, that the Christian is fitted for the work of praying with the people of God, to their edification and with comfort to himself. If there is a want of the spirit of prayer, there is great power, as we have already observed, in the exercise of family prayer to call it forth and nourish it to lively vigour. To improve the character and increase the number of our prayer-meetings, and thus advance the cause of true piety among our people, is thus one of the many modes by which the family may prove subservient to the church.

SEC. V. *The family prepares officers for the Church.*

The proper religious training of children prepares them to be officers of the church. In most of our churches, we think it may be safely said, that the majority of our elders and deacons are sons of pious parents. This, indeed, might be presumed to be the case, in view of the remarks already made, on the influence exerted by early religious training on the subsequent developments of Christian character. We know no better mode of impressing on others our own convictions on this topic, than by citing a few well authenticated facts, which may also serve to repel the repeated and foolish charge, that the children of ministers and other pious persons, more frequently continue to lead ungodly lives, than those of other persons. In our Theological Seminaries it has been so often found, on actual enumeration, that the great majority of candidates for the ministry were sons of Christian parents, that such may now be generally presumed to be true. In one institution, it was ascertained, that, at one time, five-sixths of the students had been blessed with parents, both of whom were pious, and nearly every one of the remaining sixth, had either a pious father or mother. In another, out of about fifty students, but one was found, neither of whose parents was a member of the church, and, in that case, the piety of his deceased mother had always been to her friends, a subject of just and pleasing hope. In the same seminary, at one time, it was noticed, that one third of the students were sons of ministers. Of one hundred ministers whose biographical sketches appear in Dr. Sprague's "Annals," there were as many as one hundred and ten sons, who entered the same profession. A few years ago, Dr. Alexander stated in his treatise on Family Worship, "There is a blessed instance in our own communion of six living preachers of the gospel, all sons of one man, himself a servant of the sanctuary." In an address before the Synod of Pittsburgh, by the Rev. Loyal Young, he says, "In this Synod was a devoted servant of the sanctuary, whose father, two uncles, and a brother, were also ministers, and four of whose sons are this day ministering before God. * * * Nine ministers in one family in three generations!" We know a family connection, the ancestor of which, five sons, a son-in-law, three grandsons, and two grandsons-in-law, in all twelve persons, have belonged to this sacred profession, of whom ten are now living. From an elder of one of the oldest Virginia churches, who died about sixty years since, have descended eleven ministers, and nine ministers' wives, giving a total of twenty ministers in one family connection, in three generations. That which is pleasing to observe in this case, is the fact, that the numbers belonging to the several generations, show that the blessing of God on religious culture has continued to increase, with the widening circle of descendants. Of the twenty ministers, the first generation furnished one; the second, eight; and the third, eleven. Of that third generation, there are now also several candidates for the ministry. From the same elder, have also descended eight or ten elders, and wives of elders. It deserves remark also that, humanly speaking, the influences under the direct operation of which most of these results seem to have been produced, may be traced immediately to the existence of religion in the family of the venerable elder; and as an apt illustration of our remark on the combined working of the pulpit and the family constitution, we may add, that this elder and his wife were converts under the ministry of Rev. Samuel Davies, neither having previously enjoyed (so far as can be now learned) the privileges of evangelical preaching or the influence of Christian education.

Doubtless, the family histories of Scotland, and our own country, would furnish a volume of as pleasing confirmations of the views we have presented, as any now adduced. Our God is a covenant-keeping God, and this is the covenant which he has revealed, and to which he has set the seal by his providential dealings, "My Spirit that is upon thee and my words which I have put in thy mouth, shall not depart out of thy mouth, nor out of the mouth of thy seed, nor out of the mouth of thy seed's seed, saith the Lord, from henceforth and for ever." Isa. lix. 21. Let us perform our part, and God will assuredly be faithful to his gracious promises.

CHAPTER V.

THE VALUE, DIFFICULTIES, AND AIDS TO FAMILY RELIGION.

THE family constitution is not necessarily a blessing. The head of the household may prove unfaithful to his trust, and negligent of his duties, or tyrannical and cruel in his government, and both the teacher and example of wickedness, to those of his own house. The wife may be petulant, untidy, and wasteful; children, obstinate and unruly; and servants refractory, sullen, and disorderly. So also the constitution of civil society is not always a source of blessing. Rulers may be tyrants. Judges may pervert justice. Law may be used as the instrument of oppression. The subjects of government may rebel, and the means devised for their welfare be perverted to their injury. Even the church may be perverted from that holy end for which God designed it, to be an engine of destructive power to those very interests, which it was adapted to promote. Its ministers may become the ministers of Satan, its doctrines be corrupted, or set aside by the traditions of men, and the authority of its glorified Head be employed by hypocritical officers, ruling in his name, to sustain their frauds, violence, and oppression.

The evils which have thus arisen from institutions, designed and adapted to promote human welfare, have been often ascribed, by self-conceited men, to the institutions themselves. Hence they have proposed those various methods of reconstructing society, which have been known as Communism, Socialism, and Agrarianism. Hence the schemes of the so called "Women's Rights" faction, and many other mischievous or ridiculous plans for ameliorating man's condition. We might show how all these schemes are necessarily failures, owing to the false proposition on which they rest, that man is naturally free from sin, or, as negatively stated, is not naturally depraved. As they fail to take account of man's depravity as sufficiently explaining the evils flowing from the perversion of good institutions, so they fail to recognize its cure, as essential to their methods of reformation. They propose to reform society in masses, to subject men in companies to the working of some great moral machine. They undertake to correct great evils by law; and to change public sentiment by a course of lectures, or a bushel of memorials. It has been well said, that "the kingdom of this world's morality cometh with observation." Now such is not God's plan. As in the natural, so in the moral world, he works changes by that mighty power of littles of which we before spoke. The opinion of the public, which we call public sentiment, is that of the individuals making up the public. The reformation of the public must be a reformation of persons.

The gospel is the great instrument of reform. It provides for the renewal of individuals. The moral change which it produces in any one case, may appear no great matter to any, except the subject of that change. But such a change passes on a hundred, or on thousands, and thus whole communities and states are affected. The prosperity and happiness of any one person may not be a great matter, beyond his immediate circle, but when hundreds or thousands share the same blessing, the interests of nations become improved.

Again, every man is related to others. His personal, moral change, or his prosperity and happiness, will affect the interests of others. Still the work is a work of detail. By the combination of these many particular changes and the influences which flow from them, both separately and in combination, the great reforms of the world are to be produced.

SEC. I. *The value of religion in the family.*

It is according to the foregoing suggestions, that we learn how to estimate the value of religion in the family. The piety of each of its members makes, in the aggregate, the piety of the family. True piety is the only reliable foundation of true happiness, and thus a happy home is made; and an aggregate of happy homes makes a happy community or state.

I. It is needless to enter on an elaborate discussion, to show that the evils to which we have adverted, as flowing from either of the institutions mentioned above, the family, the state, or the church, are ascribed to the sins of the persons belonging to such institutions. The desired remedy for such evils is to be found, not by the reconstruction of the institution to which they pertain, but by the reformation of the persons whose sinful conduct has produced them. True piety, as already intimated, (Ch.

II. Sect. I.,) is essential to the prevention of such evils, and also to secure to the members of the family the full benefits arising from the provisions of its constitution.

1. The simple propensities which belong to human nature, unchecked by Divine grace, will be developed in the family as well as elsewhere. For such development, indeed, the peculiar relations of the members of a family will often give special occasion. It is true that natural instincts and the relationship of protector and dependent, supply incentives to much that is praiseworthy in parents, children, and servants. Still there are many wicked passions, which these causes are unable to curb. Whether they are excited by peculiarity of relation or not, they are found to exist. The head of a family may, in some cases, be tempted to abuse his authority. This may be occasioned by a demand, in particular cases, for its stern and rigorous exercise. Power is dangerous. He is entrusted with it for the good of the whole. He is liable to forget others, and seek his own ease and comfort at their expense. The wife may be misled to question her husband's wisdom, and so repel his control in her general course of life, because she has, now and then, found good reason for believing him in error. Servants and children may presume on occasional, perhaps improper indulgences, to seek exemption from proper restraint or manifest rebellious tempers. It is not to be expected, in this present state of imperfection, that the tenderest ties of natural affection will never be strained, and the stream of pure love never be polluted, with some of the foul out-pourings of the natural heart. Distrust, jealousy, variance, disputings, heart-burnings, evil surmisings,

anger, moroseness, and obstinacy, will sometimes be developed. Strifes, alienations, bitter words, and sour looks will be found among those of kindred blood and residing under the same roof. Now, not only do the sacred precincts of the family circle forbid the intrusion of the agents of human law, for the regulation of domestic intercourse, but there are evils which human law cannot reach. That can only take cognizance of acts. It has no power to discern motives. But much of the sinfulness, which mars the beauty and destroys the happiness of the family, is consistent with a fair exterior. Many is the petty tyrant, who, while crushing the spirit of a gentle wife, or embittering the lives of children and servants with a hard bondage, has worn a gentle, quiet demeanour. Many is the wife, who, for years has practised deception on a confiding husband, and yet has preserved before spectators, the character of honesty and sincerity. Many is the youth apparently affectionate and obedient, over whose truculent behaviour, parents have wept bitter tears, in secret. Many is the servant, even, whose deceit and cunning have misled his master to blame and punish others for his own misdeeds.

But when human law is called on for relief from the evils which sin may have produced in a family, and the long concealed domestic distempers are exposed, how impotent is the law to bring relief! It can threaten,—it can punish. For any means it may possess to produce reform, the application will have been too late. The misery which has grown up so great, as to demand exposure, has become irremediable by its provisions. The agony of the Jewish parents, who felt compelled to bring their rebellious son before the judges, was but the climax of a long season of untold miseries. Days and years of ill-concealed suspicions, distrust, jealousy, recriminations, and bitter revilings, precede the dismal hour, when husband appears against wife, or wife against husband, at the tribunal of justice, demanding divorce. How many long months of anxiety, alternate remonstrance and forgiveness, insults and reconciliations, may grieved parents and a profligate son spend, ere the outraged father disinherits the boy on whose birth he once smiled!

Now, to reach the sinful tempers and correct the sinful conduct, which thus destroy the peace and neutralize the benefits of the family constitution, human law is powerless. Even when permitted to intrude into the family circle, it cannot restore its broken harmony. But where the law of man may not enter, or entering, fail to effect relief, the law of God can enter. It may appear in the household to enlighten the conscience, with condemning power, hush up excuses, and directed by the Spirit, convince of sin and humble the heart. It is followed by the gospel which can give peace to the troubled conscience, by giving peace with God through faith in Christ, and impart a renewing and sanctifying power.

2. The word and Spirit of God not only hinder the growth and check the exercise of evil passions, by the restraints which they impose, but they also provide the most effectual antidote to evil, and remedy for the disease of sin, by the new heart and right spirit which they give. We have already seen that the duties of the various members of the family are only properly performed, when they are performed under the influence of Chris-

tian principle. None are ever free from the remains of indwelling corruption while in this world, yet the change which God effects by his word and Spirit, leads its subjects "to die unto sin more and more, and live unto righteousness." The relations of the family, which, in the unregenerate state of its members, were occasions of sin, become under the operation of God's Spirit, occasions of increase in the graces of the Spirit. Love, joy, meekness, long suffering, patience, and gentleness, grow up by the exercise of the renewed soul, amid the trials of every-day life, and they re-act in the production of their kind.

Thus we learn, that true piety is the sure foundation for the purity and power of the family constitution. Its value to the household is proportioned to the evils which it prevents, and the blessings of peace and prosperity which it brings. The habits of life which are so desirable for all the members of the family to cultivate for their individual and common benefit, for time, are just those, which the religion of the gospel inculcates. Industry, order, peace, obedience, just government, honest and faithful services, are the fruits of the fear of God. A family in which the principles of piety abound, will be a prosperous and happy family. They furnish the elements of happiness which are not elsewhere to be found. Wealth may buy fields, add farm to farm, build elegant mansions, garnish them with costly furniture, procure downy beds, rich viands, sumptuous apparel, and provide means of entertainment and improvement in travel, and varied amusements, and literary advantages. But it cannot buy happiness. Moroseness may be found on sofas, contention may embitter the richest feasts. Ill-nature may stalk through splendid halls, jealousy and envyings may travel over land and seas, and discontent and animosities dwell amidst the refinements of luxury and in the libraries of learning. The health and outward prosperity of a family, though great blessings, will not ensure happiness. If the mind is ill at ease, and the heart worn with sinful passions, the greatest success in business will fail to gratify, and health of body will afford no satisfaction. Into the best ordered household, affliction will intrude. Honoured parents must wax old and feeble, and descend to the grave. Perhaps, sickness and death seize on blooming youth or prattling childhood. Reverses of fortune may come. In such hours of sorrow, the religion of the gospel alone offers a sure consolation. "Is any afflicted, let him pray." The members of the stricken household are not left to the vain and hollow language of condolence under sorrow, which is all that the world has to offer. They know in whom they have believed. The death that has entered the dwelling, is but the messenger of a Father in heaven. It may have taken a father from earth, but the widow and orphans know who is "the Father of the fatherless," and "the God of the widow." While the tears of a natural grief are flowing for the dead, faith looks beyond the tomb, and with confidence and joy, points to reunion in heaven. Even by the cold remains of the mother of his children, the bereaved husband finds consolation in the assurance, that God has sent that heaviest of all his earthly sorrows, as the chastisement of a Father, who is too wise to err, and too gracious to afflict without reason.

We do not say that religion in the family is an insurance against poverty. Yet it is true, that the truly pious family is seldom reduced to utter destitution. God is, however, often pleased to permit his people to feel, that this world is not their home, by allowing them to meet reverses in fortune, or to fail in such accumulations, as exempt them from all hardships and suffering in their outward estate. But religion brings contentment, which "with godliness is great gain." It brings a good conscience, which, itself, is full compensation for the richest luxuries of ill-gotten wealth. It brings hopes for the future, which sustain under the heaviest ills of the present. Often also, acting on the energies and elevating the moral character, it disposes to vigorous enterprise, and secures the confidence of others; so that the pious frequently retrieve their lost estates, while others sink in despair or become the victims of vice.

We are well aware, that there are many families, in which true piety does not dwell, who yet enjoy much of that family peace and order, prosperity and happiness, which we have ascribed to the power of religion in the households of the pious. But this fact rather confirms than weakens our estimate of the value of religion in the family. In such cases, the general influence of the principles of true piety may operate, although the members of the household have not personally experienced its power. Their blessings have come to them reflected, as it were, from others. Those virtues which distinguish such families are Christian virtues, in a modified form. They are the fruits of the Christian system of truth, whose power will be felt in a Christian land. If the partial operation of that system produces such benefits, what may its full influence effect? If we wish to test the results of dispensing with religion in the family, we must make our investigations in heathen lands. There we shall discover in the utter destitution of domestic virtues, the degradation of woman, the cruel tyranny of man, and the miseries and wretchedness of helpless children, the value of religion in the family.

II. Happy homes make a happy state. That happiness which implies a measure of worldly prosperity, is but the result of that purer happiness, which springs up in renewed hearts. Were all the members of all families actuated by the principles of true piety, the whole land would be enjoying the blessings of a true reformation. Thus the true method to secure national blessings, both in the destruction of vice and the promotion of virtue, is to secure family blessings.

We have already spoken of the value of religion in the family to the Church. We need therefore say the less as to its value to the State. For the members of the one are citizens of the other. Still the topic is too interesting and instructive, to be passed over without a few hints.

1. Families, reared under Christian influences, provide a healthy population. This is the true capital of a nation. This is needed to fill the ranks of the army, man the navy, fell the forests, till the land, build roads, erect cities, construct and employ machinery, and carry on the great enterprises of commerce. The nation, however, not only needs able men, but industrious, active, energetic men. True religion is a foe to idleness and indolence,

and from well trained households, go forth the recruits to the ranks of useful labour, with the hand and the head. Not only will the incentives to effort, which the wants of a family supply to its head, urge him to active effort; but the principles of true piety will induce him to train his children to useful occupation. As population is the capital, so productive labour is the income of a nation. And the mighty resources of the wealthiest people are but the aggregates of those of individuals. The pampered children of luxury and prodigality born to consume the fruits of the earth, are but the blots and blanks on the pages of a nation's history, while the well trained sons of honest industry form the material for its glory and renown.

2. Christian families provide law-abiding citizens, faithful agents, and upright rulers. The child trained to obey parents, is thus trained to obey magistrates. The citizen of the household of faith is the best citizen for the commonwealth. The habits of self-denial, generosity, forbearance, good temper, order, peace, truthfulness, and honesty, in which he has been trained, will lead him to be just in his dealings, public spirited, submissive to law, quiet and contented, peaceful and faithful. He will not be contentious, a wrangler, deceitful, dishonest, intriguing, and quarrelsome. The elements of mobs and insurrections and riots, the inmates of penitentiaries, and the subjects for the hangman, do not come out of Christian families. Mechanics, pilots, engineers, merchants, artisans, and even day labourers, who are entrusted, more or less, with the lives, or property, or material interests of others, may be fully capable in knowledge, or skill, or physical ability, and yet, if destitute of moral

principle, may fail of success. Now it is no small matter, that such should be well trained in Christian households. And it deserves the serious attention of all concerned, to inquire whether those who are prepared to disobey God, by violating the Sabbath in the service of men, may not either by the loss of physical vigour which often follows such service, or the want of moral principle, jeopard the interests of employers and the public.

The best school for rulers is the school of obedience. The principles of honesty, integrity, truthfulness, and faithfulness, which fit men for the duties of common life, are as indispensable to fit them for the highest places of authority. Incorruptible judges, virtuous statesmen, conscientious lawyers, upright jurors, truthful witnesses, honest tax-gatherers, are the proper produce of Christian families. Even generals and captains in the navy make better servants of the country by being God-fearing men. The greatest difference observable in Washington and Napoleon, was the difference in moral character. Washington's mother said, "George was always a good boy." Napoleon's education, however complete for the camp or the helm of state, left him deficient in moral principle. Whether the snows of Russia or the armies of England be most entitled to the credit of his downfall, in the view of the historian, the moralist can hardly avoid connecting it with that same overleaping ambition which led him to repudiate the wife of his heart for the empress of his dominions.

3. As national wealth is the aggregate of individual, Christian families contribute to it, both by their influence on the industrial interests of the country, and their power

to sustain themselves. All the common virtues, of which we have spoken, enter into the composition of character which secures success in life. Every self-sustaining family adds to the public wealth by diminishing public burdens. The bulk of paupers and recruits for almshouses are the vicious or their victims. The Christian family may be needy, but it is seldom entirely dependent on charity. The honest, hard working Christian man, though poor, who rears his family to be independent and also to habits of frugality, enterprise, and thrift, is a public benefactor, worth more to the state than a dozen brawling pot-house demagogues or partisan editors. Let our constitutions be destroyed, our capitols burned, our rulers driven off, and anarchy take the place of a well ordered government; yet, if our land were still covered over with Christian households, all this framework of government might be easily restored. But destroy our Christian families and those which are reared and governed by Christian principles, and let the sacred words, home, husband, wife, father, mother, brother, sister, master, and servant become obsolete, marriage be despised, authority discarded, and the ties of the family sundered; then would the wisest laws be of no avail; anarchy and tyranny would run wildly over our land, bruising with the heel and blasting with the breath the growth of a Christian civilization now rising to bless an admiring world. The value of religion in the family would be seen in the downfall of our greatness, and on the ruins of this mighty empire might be inscribed "Lo! this was a nation which feared not God!"

Sec. II. *The difficulties of Family Religion.*

On this topic we shall offer but a few hints. The leading obstacles in the way of promoting family piety have already been intimated, in stating the duties of the various members of the household, or will properly be detailed in discussing the pleas for the neglect of such duties.

1. Many parents find themselves very much embarrassed, in an honest effort to train up their children in the way of the Lord, by the habits of their neighbours. Some are addicted to Sunday visiting, and annoy a Christian family with unseasonable attentions. The children of such parents, unused to restraints or religious teachings, may, perhaps, address to those of a Christian household, the language of sneers and ridicule, and mischievously endeavour to excite them to rebel against parental authority. That fort is in danger where assailants have allies within its enclosure; so children of Christian parents, whose hearts are naturally predisposed to reject authorities and cast off restraint, are in great danger of falling an easy prey to those who endeavour to draw them aside. This difficulty often arises, also, from the associations of children in boarding-schools, where they are removed from the inspection of parents, and that constantly restraining and correcting influence, which daily association with them at home, and the weekly recurring Sabbath lessons might produce. The shame of singularity in that which is right, while there may be a glorying in being the "inventor" and leader "of evil things," is one of the sad evidences of man's alienation from God. Many parents have found the instructions of years almost effaced from the hearts of their children,

by not using proper means to prevent the existence or influence of the difficulty arising from evil associates among children. It is sometimes very difficult to regulate those associations. Happily in our country we have no privileged orders. The vulgar affectation of aristocracy of family or wealth, in which some indulge, is a ridiculous folly, for which it is hard to be charitable. Still, there may, and ought to be, distinctions in society, based on moral worth. To make such distinctions in the selection of the company of children, requires the exercise of a sound discretion, lest by reason of their natural rashness and imprudence of speech, they involve themselves and parents in trouble. Parents may do much to secure the desired object by cultivating the friendship and intercourse of families, containing children of suitable character, and in selecting schools, whose teachers are pious, and will have a wise regard to the character and influence of their pupils.

2. But there are many adult persons who give rise to great difficulties, hindering the proper influence of family religious teaching. Thus there are some thoughtless, and yet good natured friends, who show much mistaken kindness to children and youth, by allowing them, when their visitors, privileges and indulgences, which are forbidden at home. They may even comment on, what they term, the needless strictness of parental control. Sometimes we find a class of men and women who seem to take delight in producing mischief. They are gossips, and spend their time in retailing rumours.

They not only exercise a pernicious influence on children, by affecting their minds with distrust of religious friends, but they may sow seeds of jealousy and dissension in the minds of husbands and wives, or mislead masters as to servants, or servants as to masters. Among such too, are often found those, who are not only the captives, but servants of Satan, and who go about seeking whom they may mislead. They may not traduce religion, as they understand it, or vilify and slander its professors as hypocrites. On the contrary, they profess great reverence for the Bible. But the doctrines which they receive, are of a loose, undefined character, and the duties they profess to regard as most important, are of a questionable morality, or a mere compliance with some specious formalism. They are enemies of creeds, confessions, and catechisms, and all those Scripture truths, which most exalt God and humble man. They have certain set, stale speeches, about the amiability of human nature and a liberal Christianity. The moral influence of the drama, and the benefits of such innocent amusements, as card-playing and dancing, and the pleasures of genteel flirtations, intrigues, and dram-drinking are their favourite topics. Such persons are oftener found in our large towns and cities, but there are less to be feared, because better known, and parents can more easily guard their children against their wiles. They often appear in villages and rural districts, where they are not well known, and by the influence of those factitious aids, derived from the dress and manners of city or foreign life, often exert a most pernicious power in undoing, on the minds of youth, the good work of parental training.

In new settlements, where sound religious public sentiment has not yet gained an ascendency, the youth of Christian households, and, indeed, all its members are subjected to the influence of evil associates, who may not designedly do them an injury, but whose character is unworthy of imitation, and whose intercourse is either profane, or wholly worldly. The staple of their conversation is the discussion of fights, quarrels, betting, card-playing, drinking, the theatre, horse-race, and circus. Their language is grammatically as vulgar, as their sentiments are immoral. Those, who, in the selection of new homes, make their choice, solely in view of the advantages of making money, often sacrifice the more important privileges of their families, in respect of moral and mental improvement. It would be better to live on harder fare and accumulate less property, than to rear wealthy families, grown up under the droppings of Satan's ministrations.

For all such difficulties as have been noticed, parents must prepare, by the more careful teaching of their children, by special warnings, and by attaching them to themselves. They must early accustom their children to repose implicitly on their counsel, and endeavour to make home replete with attractive means of happiness. Let them aim to preoccupy the heart with good, as the best means of excluding evil influences, whether from playmates, godless companions, sceptical teachers, or imprudent neighbours. Let them not be discouraged by those or other difficulties, arising from the perverseness of children or servants, the innate opposition of the heart to religious truth, or the natural volatility and fickleness of youth. No valuable result is ever attained without the use of appropriate means and the exertion of great diligence, unwearied watchfulness, and unfailing perseverance. Those who find difficulties in their own tempers, or in the varied tempers and dispositions of children, are already instructed in the best means to be employed for their removal. All who wish to know and do their duty, will find all needed grace, if they seek it from the Father of mercies, and the God of all grace and consolation.

SEC. III. *The aids to Family Religion.*

1. Corresponding to the class of difficulties, of which we have chiefly spoken, is the aid by which parents may be assisted in their holy work, afforded by good associates. Such, among children, are often found in the families of the pious, of whatever position in society. But, as even the best children are not always entirely reliable, parents ought to be careful to ascertain the character of the influence exerted on their own children by those of others. By proper training, young persons may themselves be led, at a very early age, to be good judges of the character of those with whom they associate.

But the aid of good company is to be sought, rather from the association in families of adults, whose literary and moral advantages and attainments will make their conversation edifying, and their examples worthy of imitation. Parental preferences will greatly influence those of children. As reading biography is exceedingly interesting and improving to the young, so associating with good men and women cannot fail to exercise a wholesome influence in the formation of their characters. It is peculiarly important, that persons of decided Christian character should be thus brought into their society. They will learn that the idle talk of worldlings and the flippant jests of coxcombs and flirts respecting such persons are unfounded, and be led to admire Christianity in the persons of those who exemplify its principles. As youth grow up to adult age, they will continue to prefer such companions, and their influence on their settlement in life will continue to be salutary, leading to proper connections in business or marriage, judicious selections of a home, and wise plans for the whole course of life.

2. The work of religious instruction in the family derives great aid from well conducted Sabbath-schools. These schools are not designed to be substitutes for home teaching, when parents are capable of performing their duties. That too many thus misuse them, has led some to depreciate their value. But this is wrong. Rather let the fault of parents be checked. Such institutions are too valuable, as supplying the only means of religious instruction to thousands of destitute children, to be discarded, because indolent, self-indulgent parents choose to devolve on others their own peculiar duties.

But while continuing as zealously as ever to instruct children at home, parents can derive valuable aid to regularity and system, so important in all departments of instruction, by making the Sabbath-school lesson, at least in part, the home lesson also. Thus will the child not only be more certainly prepared for the duties of the class, but he will be incited and encouraged by having the care and interest of parents manifested in his behalf. The support thus given to the teacher's authority and instructions, will be also some just compensation for his self-denying and arduous labour.

The aid of the Sabbath-school is valuable also to the older children, who, by engaging in its duties, as teachers, continue to improve in Divine knowledge, and acquire early habits of usefulness and benevolence. The Sabbath-schools for servants will afford a field of special advantage to all, who will engage in the laudable effort to give them religious instruction.

3. We most cheerfully recognize our excellent religious newspapers, and the publications of our Board, as most valuable and efficient helps in training a family in the knowledge and love of true piety. Of the latter, we have now a large number and variety, well adapted to the wants of all the members of a family, and especially the younger. So all the families in our church can be supplied, on very moderate terms, with religious newspapers, edited by some of our most eminent ministers. In all such, there has been introduced, of late years, a special department, called the "Children's Column;" and then the Board of Publication issues a paper entirely devoted to their instruction and entertainment.

The judicious use of these books and newspapers is attended with manifest advantage to the intellectual and moral improvement of youth. A well edited paper of any kind is a great blessing to the children of a family, by inducing them to form habits of reading. They may also gather an immense amount of useful knowledge. Especially, do religious newspapers confer great benefits; for, to the mental improvement, they add high moral influences. Children, habituated to such reading, have their minds familiarized with the truths, which they hear from the pulpit, read in the Bible, or learn from parents. They become instructed in the condition and plans of the church, and its growth and agency in disseminating the gospel, and may be thus led to take a more lively interest in the prosperity of Zion. Above all, the solemn truths on the subject of personal religion, so often found in such papers, may be attended by the awakening and renewing power of the Divine Spirit.

Parents should use a wise discretion in selecting books for the perusal of children, adapted to their age and progress in knowledge. They also need to attend to their manner of reading. Children are fond of novelty, and constantly tempted to read carelessly. They may glance through a volume, merely for the sake of the story it may contain, neglecting the solid instruction to which the story is the mere attraction. They will thus grow up with very bad habits of reading in a hurried or careless manner. They ought, therefore, to be induced to read aloud to some one, who will correct their errors of elocution; and should be frequently examined on the contents of the books which they may have perused.

Before leaving this subject, we may remark, that persons benevolently disposed, may contribute materially to aid poor families in the right training of children, by supplying them with religious books and newspapers. Even many who can afford to procure them, but are indifferent to their value, when furnished for a time by others, might become sufficiently interested to supply themselves. While a direct benefit would be conferred on the objects of this benevolent action, an incidental and valuable service would be performed to a class of laborious and useful Christian men, who, amidst much annoyance and discouragement, and on very inadequate remuneration, are engaged in editing and publishing religious newspapers.

4. Our families cannot always continue in health, comfort, and peace. Sickness, losses, bereavements, and death are incidental to all households. But even these sad events may be properly employed as aids to impress the great principles of religious truth on the hearts of all in the household. They are sent to confirm the lessons of God's word, on the vanity of life, the transitory nature of earthly enjoyments, and the value, reality, and permanence of heavenly blessings. Their teaching is sad, but not the less valuable. It is often "better to go to the house of mourning than to the house of feasting," and "by the sadness of the countenance the heart is made better." Sometimes that great calamity, orphanage, is overruled to be the source of blessing to children. Their early acquaintance with the sad realitites of life, produces a seriousness of disposition and proper views of their responsibilities, and gives a direction to energies, which other, more pleasing, methods might have failed to effect. Let us not "despise the chastening of the Lord," as an aid to us, in guiding our children, as well as tutoring ourselves, in the way of life. Often it is true, that

> The path of sorrow, and that path alone,
> Leads to the world where sorrow is unknown.

CHAPTER VI.

THE PLEAS FOR NEGLECT AND DELINQUENCIES IN FAMILY DUTIES.

THE instincts of nature and self-interest generally secure a good measure of faithfulness in the performance of those duties, which relate to the physical and mental interests of the members of a family. When any neglect occurs, the fault is often ascribable to ignorance, or to an inadequate apprehension of the benefits which may be procured by the performance, or the evils which may result from the omission, of duty. In such cases instruction and admonition are appropriate. When, however, there exists any culpable and pertinacious disregard of the obligations to provide for the physical welfare or mental improvement of children, it will probably be found, that the excuses offered in extenuation or justification of such omissions, are substantially those by which a neglect of the moral and religious training of a family is usually palliated. Indeed, if this latter work be properly performed, the other will rarely be omitted, on any such grounds as demand our notice in this connection.

Few persons, whose opinions are entitled to respect, will question the manifest and manifold advantages of religion in the family. Christianity enjoys this distinguishing peculiarity, as a system of religion, that, however men may dispute its credibility, object to its doctrines, or refuse submission to its laws, they feel constrained to do homage to its principles, as illustrated in the lives of its votaries. Hence numbers can be found, who, though unwilling themselves to be pious, are far from being displeased with their friends because they profess and practise the principles of Christian faith. Prejudice, the depraved passions of the human heart, or ignorance, or all combined, may occasionally, even in our highly favoured Christian land, induce persons to oppose the religious inclinations of their near relatives ; and husbands, wives, parents, or children, have been known to evince a most bitter hostility, even leading to acts of petty persecution, against "them of their own household," who had professed faith in Christ. But even in these, now happily, rare and extreme cases, the hostility has generally been occasioned, rather by the principles than conduct of the Christian disciple.

While, however, the beauty of holiness, especially in the characters of mothers, fathers, children, brothers, or sisters, may be readily conceded, the necessity and importance of using the appropriate means to secure the admired result, are not always properly appreciated. This failure may be owing to ignorance or a want of consideration, or it is more probably oftener occasioned by the sophistical reasonings and cavils of those who are ever prepared to hinder the progress of true piety in the world.

Even when the duty of employing such means is professedly acknowledged, many permit themselves to be hindered in its performance by the suggestions of indolence, or the natural indisposition of the heart, to enter with zeal and energy on the fulfilment of moral obligations.

1. Some undertake to justify their neglect of parental duty, in the religious culture of children, by the allegation that the opinions of the young on subjects of Christian faith ought not to be biassed, but that they should be left to exercise their own judgments on matters of such importance, when they shall have reached a period of life, at which they may be capable of acting for themselves.

(1.) This plea sometimes aspires to the dignity of an objection, on the ground, that if the alleged duty is obligatory on any, it is one of common obligation, and that, when performed by parents, who are zealous partisans of religious error, it becomes the instrument of propagating such error, and thus of doing evil instead of good.

We cannot deny, that, in view of the great injury inflicted on mankind, by the various systems of false religion and perverted Christianity, which have been instilled into the tender and susceptible minds of youth, there is some plausibility in this view when first presented. Still we think that it will be found only plausible.

For, admitting that, by early religious instruction, many have been led astray and made the victims of pernicious error, it remains to be proved, that, if not thus instructed, they would have embraced the truth. And even granting that moral interests have thus been often sacrificed, we must bear in mind that the wrong application of a good principle is not a sound reason for its rejection. We have often had occasion to advert to the fact that the Divine government of this world is a government of sinful beings, and must not be held responsible for the perversion of its wise provisions, which are made by the folly and wickedness of men. At every turn we shall meet this same difficulty. Even the restraints of God's holy law, the apostle teaches us, have been made the occasions of sin by the perverseness of the human heart. Rom. vii. 8.

But we can by no means admit that the moral interests of a child are necessarily sacrificed, who has been placed under a system of religious instruction, by which some error has been inculcated. For the most defective system, taught by any evangelical denomination of the Protestant church, may contain enough truth to produce a saving influence, under the divine blessing. Even in papal countries, with all the prevailing superstitions and the infidelity engendered by them, some religious benefits may be secured by the religious instruction given, which presents a pleasing contrast to the condition of one left in a state of utter ignorance of Divine truth. We by no means advocate indifference as to the system of religious faith, under which children are reared, and yet, there might be cases, in which it would be better for children to be brought up under the tuition of a Christless Unitarianism or Universalism, or even Judaïsm itself, than that they should be left to be the prey of the devil, under the leadings of their own depraved natures. We are well aware of the great difficulty which the prejudiced attachment to error, interposes to the entrance of truth; yet as all error is only a form of sin, it may, at least, admit of a doubt, whether we would not do better to risk the mingling of error with some truth, than to leave the mind, fully preoccupied with sinful propensities, in the darkness of an utter ignorance of Divine revelation.

(2.) The alleged impolicy of a religious education is partly based on the presumption, that the mind of a child, if not inclined to what is good, is naturally unbiassed, and will as readily select what is right, as that which is wrong. But that such is by no means a correct view of our nature, both Scripture and a discriminating observation abundantly prove. We need only refer to the first and third chapters of the Epistle to the Romans, as presenting a summary of the inspired declarations on this subject, which other portions of the Bible fully corroborate. The universal and total depravity of the race is the only theory of man's moral nature, consistent with those facts of his history, patent in all the records of the race, that the peace and order of society, safety of life and property, the dispensation of justice and the practice of truth, have never been secured, except by the restraints of law and the curbs of government.

So far, then, from being disposed by nature, to that which is right, or even indisposed to that which is wrong, the child is already "wholly inclined to all evil," "disabled," and naturally opposed to all that is good, born with a propensity to imbibe erroneous principles and pursue sinful practices. This corrupt nature, left to an unchecked development, is not merely the source of all "actual transgression," (Confession of Faith, vi. 4,) but it is the source of ungodliness and transgression only, "and that continually." It is a sheer folly to admonish us against the dangers of a religious bias, when there already exists a sinful bias, and the power of Satan, and the delusions of a wicked world are constantly engaged to strengthen its force.

(3.) But if the plea now before us possesses any validity to justify the neglect of that religious education, for which we have contended in the foregoing chapters, it may be urged, with as much plausibility, if not equal pertinency, to justify a neglect of every kind and measure of religious or moral teaching. The practical principles of sound morality are sustained by the fundamental doctrines of revealed truth. We need not here discuss this proposition. That there may have existed imperfect codes of morals, in lands on which the light of the gospel never shone, is true. But, we shall search in vain, in all the records of our race, for a system so complete, as that which rests on the doctrines of the word of God. A comparison of the moral condition of the most enlightened ancient or modern heathen nation, with that of Christian nations, in which the most imperfect forms of Christianity have prevailed, will show, that the latter have enjoyed the benefits of a much sounder morality than the former.

Now such doctrines of revealed religion as the being and nature of God, man's responsibility, the state of rewards and punishments hereafter, are doctrines which men do not receive by nature, and for the right apprehension of which they need instruction. For even granting that men will, as well as may, know the "eternal power and Godhead," by the "things which are seen," (Rom. i. 20,) still it is notorious, that all have not followed the light of nature. The heathen needed instructers in its teachings, and among the most enlightened nations of the heathen world atheism has existed. Then there must be religious teaching as to some truths. Indeed, without it, we could easily show that the whole world must ultimately drift to a state of most deplorable darkness. If no religious training must be given on propositions, which may be subjects of debate, lest we unduly bias the mind and invade the rights of conscience, then might society soon be deprived of the benefits arising from the sanction of an oath. If children are to be left without instruction in the doctrine of the existence of God, we know not how soon that would become as much doubted and rejected, as the petty dogmas of some mere sectarian policy. So all the questions of morals involving the safety of life and the rights of property, must follow the doctrines of revealed religion, in being placed among the topics on which instruction must be declined, because they admit of debate. We cannot contemplate with equanimity, the prospect of a nation, left to the full consequences which must flow from the practical admission of the plea, which we are now considering. It is said, that Coleridge once replied to a friend, who had urged it, by showing him his garden, which had grown up in weeds, because he had neglected to "prejudice it" in favour of fruits and flowers. So, unless children are "prejudiced" in favour of religious doctrines, and the love and practice of justice, generosity, honesty, and truth, they will grow up in infidelity, and the love and practice of fraud and cruelty, hatred, revenge, and lying.

Nor is it a fair reply to these suggestions, to say that it is proper to teach those things, on which there is a general agreement among men, while those of a limited reception should be omitted from our instructions; for the popularity of a proposition in morals is not conclusive of its truth, nor the popular rejection of it, an evidence of its falsehood; and the question raised by this plea does not relate to the degree of doubt pertaining to such propositions, but to the existence of any difference of opinion whatever. If we may teach one set of truths which some question, so may we teach another. If then the Christian parent is persuaded of the truth of the religious system which he has adopted, it is both his right and duty to inculcate it on the mind of his child. If the so called prejudices are right, and such as he believes that the sound reason and enlightened conscience of the child will afterwards sanction, then, by all means, he should endeavour to preoccupy its mind with them. And this he should do, at as early a period of the child's life as possible. We all admit the importance of teaching children the arts and sciences, the principles of ordinary morality, and even the manners of polite society. And all feel, that the earlier we inculcate the lessons on these subjects the better. Early impressions are most durable, and early habits the most uneradicable. We do not wait till children can appreciate the propriety, or understand the reasons of the principles of such morals or manners. It is enough, that we feel persuaded they ought to be instructed and trained to observe them. Now, if we feel that it is right and important thus to teach them those things to which they have no natural aversion, but, on the contrary, for the learning of which they may be inclined, by a regard to their own interest, the example and influence of others, or any similar reason; how much more should we feel impelled to use every care for training them to the reception of truths, and the adoption of practices, to which they are by nature disinclined! In the former case, we may be incited to duty by a consideration of the ignorance or indolence of our children; much more then should we be moved to our duty in the latter, by bearing in mind, that we have to contend not only with ignorance and indolence, but with a decided repugnance to truth and an inveterate perverseness of heart.

2. In direct contradiction of the inspired promise, that if a child is trained up in the "way he should go, when he is old, he will not depart from it," (Prov. xxii. 6,) it has been often said, that the result produced by religious education will be the opposite to that which is proposed. We are told that children, who have been restrained from certain indulgences when young, acquire a greater desire and relish for them, when they reach adult age; and that to those religious truths which are urged on their attention, and to those outward religious duties with which they are forced to comply in early life, they will become even more strongly averse, when released from parental control.

We have really hesitated somewhat on the introduction of this excuse for neglect of parental duties, for, to some readers, it must appear exceedingly strange, that any persons can thus so openly contradict the Divine testimony. But, however shocking to pious minds this palpable insult to God may appear, we are fully persuaded that either in its bald impudence, or under the guise of some modifying expressions, this plea is often advanced. Some undertake to sustain its truth, by the repetition of the stale slander, that the children of the pious are, ordinarily, worse than those of others. A feeble attempt to reconcile the obvious contradiction of God's word which this plea presents, is offered in the suggestion, that no religious training is such as God's word requires, and hence, since our imperfect endeavours are so uniformly failures, they had better be altogether abandoned. But it is not our province to discuss this or any other method of reconciling the explicit assurances of God's word with the contradictory positions to which men may be led, either by indisposition to accept the Divine declaration, or the sophistical reasonings of themselves or others. We have long regarded the existence and use of this plea as a most striking exemplification of the inspired teaching, that "the carnal mind is enmity against God, for it is not subject to the law of God." Rom. viii. 7.

As to the alleged facts adduced to sustain the position before us, we may remark, that they have never been well authenticated. It is possible there may have been many professing Christians and ministers, who have, like Eli, been culpably remiss in duty. There have, doubtless, been some who have been too stern in rebuke, too severe in punishment, too rigorous in requisitions;

or, on the contrary, others who have been too lax in discipline, too lenient to the guilty, or too indulgent to the indolent. All have, doubtless, failed in some respect, and come short of performing acknowledged duties. Still, after much reflection and observation, we are free to express the conviction, that we find much more reason to admire the distinguishing forbearance and faithfulness of our God, in so eminently blessing the religious education of children, though conducted with so much imperfection, and fulfilling his promises, though so often forfeited by the sinful omissions of his people, than to doubt or question the truth of the inspired declaration, or the wisdom of that family economy, for which it provides both the foundation and encouragement.

On the other hand, the facts already stated may be safely relied on to repel the slanderous allegation, by which it is proposed to impugn the truth of God's word. Other facts of the same kind may be gathered from the history of the church. A few years since, some statistics were collected in New England, with special reference to this subject. From these we have selected a few statements:

Of one hundred and forty one children, fifteen years old and upwards, in the families of thirty-five ministers, about one hundred were found hopefully pious, of whom nineteen were devoted to the ministry. Only four sons were intemperate. The mother of one of them was not pious.

In the families of one hundred and seventy-two deacons,* there were seven hundred and ninety-six children,

* In the congregational churches of New England, the Deacon corresponds in office to the Ruling Elder of our churches.

fifteen years old, and upwards, of whom about five hundred were hopefully pious, and seventeen were ministers. Sixteen were intemperate. The fathers of five of these used strong drink, or opposed a temperance reform. The remaining two hundred and eighty four were, with few exceptions, respectable and useful citizens. Now let there be selected from irreligious households, in which religious training is rejected or neglected, an equal number of families and children, and we unhesitatingly assert, that like numbers of professors of religion and ministers will not be found. And even should such be found, in order to sustain the position that religious teaching is injurious, it must be further proved, that those of the first class became pious in spite of the instruction they had received; and those of the latter, by reason of the ignorance in which they had been left.

It is true that grace does not run in the blood, but God's promise is sure, and God's precept will be ever sustained by his dispensations. The kingdom of providence is subservient to the kingdom of grace. As to the alleged propensity of children, to seek with greater avidity, when of age and free from control, those indulgences from which they had been restrained in early life, we may freely concede, that there is a melancholy proclivity of our nature to rush after what is forbidden, and to hate what is productive of our best interests. It is the testimony of inspiration that "a fool" (*i. e.*, wicked person) despiseth his father's instruction," Prov. xv. 5, that "foolishness is bound in the heart of a child," Prov. xxii. 15, that "fools hate knowledge," Prov. i. 22, and "make a mock at sin." Prov. xiv. 9. But so far from admitting that these evidences of a sinful nature, should constitute a reason for omitting all efforts to inculcate a love for truth and the fear of God, they supply very strong incentives to use the utmost diligence, in our efforts for the religious culture of children. If indeed we adopt the principle, that we must omit all such efforts for fear of producing results contrary to what we propose to accomplish, then, to be consistent, we must dispense with all training, by which we propose to effect any change in the natural disposition of children. They must be left to learn the most ordinary yet most important moral duties of life, after they shall have become habituated to neglect them. Even the manners of social intercourse must be regarded as forbidden topics of parental teaching. Children must be left to rude and boorish methods of behaviour, lest the effort to teach them suavity and politeness might inspire them with a dislike to the customs of civilized society. They must be left to grow up in ignorance, lest the offered teachings of letters and useful science might be rejected with repugnance. Or, if by compulsion we should succeed in enforcing judicious counsels and restraints in such matters, and securing some progress in knowledge, we must expect, that as our sons and daughters reach the period, when, released from our control, they may indulge their pent up propensities, they will greedily resort to the vulgarities of low life, break off all the habits and usages of good society, luxuriate in indolence and idleness, and disdainfully discontinue the pursuit of all mental improvement! To escape the conclusions to which these suggestions lead, it may be said, that the alleged results of religious training do not flow from any necessary proclivity in the child's nature to oppose instruction on all subjects, but is due to their natural antipathy to religious truth. If this be so, then surely it is highly important that we use the greater zeal and diligence, not only to instil good principles, but to eradicate this deadly hostility to their reception, lest it become too deeply fixed, ever to allow their entrance in after life.

Once more, there are not a few who do, practically, oppose the instruction and discipline of youth, in any department of knowledge or duty, to which they manifest repugnance. The great bulk of children thus neglected grow up practical demonstrations of the impolicy, or rather wickedness, of such neglect. By their uncultivated manners, gross ignorance, and idle, vicious habits, they bring disgrace on parents and ruin on themselves. Some few, notwithstanding this parental folly, under the influence of society to which they are subject, may acquire propriety of behaviour, good habits of ordinary morality, and a respectable degree of mental improvement, and thus escape such sad results. But it must be considered, that while the influence of society may supply the defects of training, in the ordinary duties and decencies of life, to which children may have no very strong disinclination, or a disinclination which may be overcome by the incentives of self interest, we are not permitted to rely on similar causes and expect similar results, as to the principles and practices of a vital piety. To these, as already stated, the heart is naturally opposed, and even in the best state of society, the influences to which youth are constantly exposed, so far from tending to overcome, rather tend to increase, such disinclination. The boys in the street, wicked men and women in their homes, the example and solicitations of the votaries of sin, and the allurements of the world, of every sort, and in all the scenes of opportunity and temptation, are continually drawing children aside to evil, and opposing all the best efforts of parents to train them in the way they should go. If the garden be neglected, the soil, prolific of weeds, will be luxuriant in a noxious growth.

3. There are many special pleas urged, under the influence of peculiar circumstances, or in excuse for the neglect of particular duties, not admitting any classification, which deserve a brief notice. Such of these as relate to the great duty of family worship, are so well and so summarily disposed of in the concluding chapter of the work often cited, that, by a reference to it, we omit all farther allusion to them.

(1.) The intimacy of the family relation is often suggested, as a reason for the failure of husbands and wives to stir up each other's minds, on the great concerns of salvation, or of parents to converse with their children on the duties of personal piety. There may be a proper degree of diffidence in our abilities, to be the instructers of others, more painfully experienced, when the very solemn interests of our near and dear relatives are to be affected by our counsels. Still, it is much to be feared, that this plea has its true origin, either in a consciousness that our lives are inconsistent with our theories and professions, or that we are not sufficiently impressed with a sense of the pressing necessity of personal religion, in those who are members of our families. Sometimes indeed, there may arise a false delicacy, as if "the subject," to use a popular phraseology in denoting religious topics, were one too sacred to be made a topic of familiar conversation. We apprehend this plea, under any modification, is sufficiently set aside by the suggestion, that whenever our own piety is vigorous and active, all the real or supposed difficulties which it presents will vanish.

(2.) The plea of a want of time is sometimes presented. A similar plea for the neglect of attending to personal religion is sometimes offered. In both cases there may be a misapprehension of the nature of the duty from which exemption is thus claimed. God has so ordered that our most diligent performance of the duties pertaining to our lawful callings, is not only consistent with the special duty we owe to him, but we are very much aided in the former, by a proper regard for the latter. All the duties we are called to perform in promoting our own piety, and that of the members of our families, are effectually operating in the advancement of our best temporal interests. And even did our engagement in the religious instruction of our children, or other Christian services for our families, interfere with the prosecution of our proper secular pursuits, the transcendent value of the spiritual welfare of our household might justify a sacrifice of some worldly interest for its advantage.

(3.) Some endeavour to pacify the demands of a quickened conscience, especially in regard to the religious instruction of servants, by the plea, that religion is a matter between each person and his Maker; and that if they endeavour to serve God sincerely themselves, their children and servants know their liabilities and duties, and must take care to meet them. It is very true that each of us must give account of himself to God; but does it never occur to such persons, that a very important part of such account will be that which relates to the "deeds done in the body," in accordance with requisitions of the family constitution? We cannot be pious for others, but if God has placed us in the position of a keeper of our brother's religious privileges, it is a matter for serious consideration, that we may be held responsible for supplying him with those privileges. Masters and parents cannot devolve wholly on others, what their very relation to their servants and children has imposed on them.

(4.) In respect to the class of duties to which we have just adverted, we often hear neglect palliated on the allegation, that those whom we are called to instruct will not heed our lessons. As to both classes of pupils, children and servants, this may very probably be true, when, by our sloth and indifference, they have been allowed to form habits of inattention to serious things. But if proper means are used when they are young, we need not fear that our efforts will be rejected. Let us abide by the promise, (Prov. xxii. 6,) encouraging as to any child, whether our own or that of our servant, in this respect sufficiently subject to our control to enable us to perform the duty, on which the promise is suspended.

(5.) A want of capacity to instruct and discipline the young, is sometimes plead in excuse for neglect. "If there be first a willing mind, it is accepted according to that a man hath, and not according to that he hath not."

2 Cor. viii. 12. This principle of God's gracious government applies to our duties as well as to our gifts of benevolence. Let each one do his best. There is not, indeed, a requisition for great gifts of knowledge, to teach others the essential truths of the gospel, both as to its theory and the duties it prescribes. In this respect, this wonderful scheme for man's moral welfare resembles some vast and complicated machinery, which has been so well adjusted, that a little child may set in operation a power, which scores or hundreds of men could not, of themselves, effect. If the deficiencies of capacity are specially such as relate to temper of mind, patience, gentleness, zeal, and earnestness, they are to be supplied, like all other graces, at that throne to which we are invited to come for mercy and grace to help in time of need.

(6.) Past failure, either of ourselves or others, is no valid excuse for remitting our efforts. If it has resulted from the stupidity or stubbornness of those, who, even in early life, have evinced the dreadful perversity of human nature, let us call to mind God's long-suffering and patient forbearing toward us. If, however, it has resulted from our past delinquencies, then, indeed, should we rather be humbled and penitent, and knowing that God giveth liberally to all, and upbraideth none, seek from him forgiveness for the past, and wisdom to direct, and strength to aid us for the future; that with a livelier zeal, and a more persevering endeavour, we may be led "to do good and communicate," as we have "opportunity." Our humblest efforts will not escape his regard, and our success, so far as it shall be for his glory, will form part of that blessedness, which those shall receive, who shall hereafter enter into the joy of their Lord.

This discussion has strengthened us in convictions long entertained, and to which we fain hope it may be instrumental in leading the minds of those who may honour this little work with a perusal. We feel fully persuaded, that in addition to the diligent use of all those valuable methods, for increasing the efficiency of the gospel and enhancing the power of the pulpit, which God has inclined his people to employ, one of the most important enterprises which can now engage the attention of our ministers and church courts, is the devising and executing the best methods for promoting family religion.

Let us suppose that all the members of the hundred thousand families, reckoned to be connected with the Presbyterian church in our country, were led to feel and act as they should, in view of their responsibilities and duties as taught in the Holy Scriptures, granting all that abatement from perfection which human infirmity may require, there would yet be thus produced such a revival of pure religion as the world has never known. There would be such repentance on conviction of past short-comings, such endeavours after new obedience, such earnest inquiries for direction, such wrestlings in prayer, such exercises of faith, such returning to walk in the fear of God, as would constitute a scene, on which angels would look with joy, and for which all good men on earth would unite in praising God. It might not be a revival, distinguished by any obvious excitement, by any undue increase or multiplication of public religious meetings, by overflowing houses of disorderly curiosity-hunters; or, by accessions of large numbers to the church, to be followed by the defection of the large majority of such accessions; but it would be a steady, uninterrupted stream of spiritual blessing, consisting in the uniform growth of churches in numbers, and the uniform growth of their members in true piety; the regular increase of candidates for the ministry, the founding of new churches, the promotion of peace and order and love, the enlargement of missionary enterprises among the heathen, the weakening of the kingdom of Satan, the advancement of the kingdom of grace, and the hastening of the kingdom of glory.

For such a revival, let all who sustain positions of influence and authority in every family, earnestly labour, praying for Divine aid and blessing. Let elders stir up the minds of Christian parents, husbands, wives, masters, and older children, to a right appreciation and earnest performance of duty. Especially let us, who are called to "labour in word and doctrine," most diligently instruct the people of our charges, in the nature, importance, and duties of the family constitution, the means by which the great moral purposes of its organization may be secured, and the benefits which Christian families confer on the church, the state, and the world. Instead of seeking the enlargement of Zion by some "new measures," inconsistent with the tenor of our doctrinal system and church order, let us return to the old paths; and by the lawful use of the facilities afforded by our chosen modes of worship, and the careful instruction of our children in our chosen articles of faith, let us seek the blessing of a covenant-keeping God. Let others boast ters; or, by accessions of large numbers to the church, to be followed by the defection of the large majority of such accessions; but it would be a steady, uninterrupted stream of spiritual blessing, consisting in the uniform growth of churches in numbers, and the uniform growth of their members in true piety; the regular increase of candidates for the ministry, the founding of new churches,

www.ingramcontent.com/pod-product-compliance
Lightning Source LLC
LaVergne TN
LVHW010742120826
845150LV00009B/1400

* 9 7 8 1 4 2 5 5 1 7 3 9 7 *